Further Praise for *Journeys of Charter School Creators*

"In *Journeys of Charter School Creators*, Maria Marsella Leahy and Rebecca Ann Shore peel back the many diverse layers of leadership revealing not only lessons in school leadership but in leadership as a field of study. Successful leadership is sustained through not only extraordinarily hard work and creativity but also through a marriage-like level of devotion and commitment to a set of shared values. This book is a valuable resource for aspiring and new charter school founders, education regulators and authorizers, legislators, and even traditional public school board members. While *Journeys of Charter School Creators* focuses on charter school leadership and creativity, the memorable lessons of its subjects apply to any organization." —**Eddie Goodall**, North Carolina State Senator; founder and director, North Carolina Association of Public Charter Schools; 2018 Lifetime Achievement Award winner for extensive work with charter schools

"Whether it is an urban school like Odyssey in Pasadena, California, or a rural school set in the mountains of North Carolina like Thomas Jefferson Classical Academy, the leaders showcased in this book have one characteristic in common: they are like missionaries who have been called to serve the needs of the students in their communities. Grit and a growth mind-set are two of the most important requirements these servant-leaders possess. If you, too, have the desire to take on this Herculean task, read the book to see if you've got what it takes." —**Rhonda Dillingham**, executive director, North Carolina Association for Public Charter Schools

Journeys of Charter School Creators

Journeys of Charter School Creators

Leadership for the Long Haul

Maria Marsella Leahy
and Rebecca Ann Shore

Foreword by
Terrence E. Deal

Preface by
Guilbert C. Hentschke

ROWMAN & LITTLEFIELD
Lanham • Boulder • New York • London

Published by Rowman & Littlefield
An imprint of The Rowman & Littlefield Publishing Group, Inc.
4501 Forbes Boulevard, Suite 200, Lanham, Maryland 20706
www.rowman.com

6 Tinworth Street, London SE11 5AL, United Kingdom

Copyright © 2019 by Maria Marsella Leahy and Rebecca Ann Shore

All rights reserved. No part of this book may be reproduced in any form or by any
electronic or mechanical means, including information storage and retrieval systems,
without written permission from the publisher, except by a reviewer who may quote
passages in a review.

British Library Cataloguing in Publication Information Available

Library of Congress Cataloging-in-Publication Data

Names: Leahy, Maria Marsella, author. | Shore, Rebecca, author.
Title: Journeys of charter school creators : leadership for the long haul /
    Maria Marsella Leahy and Rebecca Ann Shore.
Description: Lanham, Maryland : Rowman & Littlefield, [2019] | Includes
    bibliographical references.
Identifiers: LCCN 2018043053 (print) | LCCN 2018045713 (ebook) |
    ISBN 9781475847017 (Electronic) | ISBN 9781475846997 (cloth : alk. paper) |
    ISBN 9781475847000 (pbk. : alk. paper)
Subjects: LCSH: Charter schools—United States–Administration. | Educational
    Leadership—United States. | School management and organization—United States.
Classification: LCC LB2806.36 (ebook) | LCC LB2806.36 .L43 2019 (print) |
    DDC 371.05—dc23
LC record available at https://lccn.loc.gov/2018043053

♾™ The paper used in this publication meets the minimum requirements of American
National Standard for Information Sciences—Permanence of Paper for Printed Library
Materials, ANSI/NISO Z39.48-1992.

Printed in the United States of America

To All Leaders & Learners,

Especially,

Alessondra, Lucia, Josie,

Lily & Bobby.

Contents

Foreword

Over the years, American Education has been shaped and reshaped by a variety of social, philosophical, and political movements. Some have left a significant mark; others have come and gone with only a whisper of a trace. One of the most significant movements in American education has been Horace Mann's Common Schools Initiative of the 1800s. This initiative promulgated compulsory attendance for all students up to an acceptable level of literacy. States were required to form local boards of education to create schools capable of achieving fundamental goals of teaching basic skills, inculcating desirable moral habits and providing opportunities for less fortunate students to succeed on par with the more advantaged. Merit, in a fluid society, would ideally trump birth.

Traces of the Common School crusade are still visible in public schools today: compulsory attendance, focus on basic skills and oversight by a locally elected school board. Over time, however, state and federal initiatives and regulations have usurped a measure of local control. Since Mann, other notables have also etched traces on public schools: John Dewey, Montessori, Bloom, and A. S. Neil. In addition, proponents of the accountability movement, measuring learning outcomes and introducing the rational emphasis of business to education organizations has, and will continue to shape how schools are run as well as viewed by external constituents.

The Alternative Schools Movement of the 1970s preceded Charter Schools. Legislation at that time waived all provisions of state education codes (except in California, earthquake provisions), and gave educators license to create schools that mirrored the social unrest of the time. Whether free-standing or district based, alternatives were almost always grassroots efforts to eliminate arbitrary discipline codes and empower students on par with teachers. Together they experimented and searched for new and better ways to learn.

In addition to their grassroots character, novel curricular and instructional patterns, Alternative Schools departed significantly from traditional patterns of organizing. Students, teachers, and often parents were given far more access to schoolwide decision making and accorded more influence than in regular public schools. Many saw the departure from bureaucratic patterns of education as a distinguishing feature of 1960s and 1970s Alternative Schools. By 1975 estimates pegged 5,000 alternative schools in the United States. This included continuation schools, learning centers, schools within schools, open schools, schools without walls, and free schools. Suppositions and testimonials credited alternatives for providing opportunities for students previously alienated from traditional patterns and ways.

Unfortunately alternatives of the 1960s and 1970s, for a variety of reasons, were unstable. Pioneers underestimated the power of social myths legitimizing traditional educational patterns. Questions about the impact of alternatives were difficult to answer. Students often had difficulty adjusting to freedom and ambiguity. Teachers questioned their roles in shaping learning options. Parents began to wonder what students were learning, if anything. As a result, many of the alternatives failed, either closing their doors or reverting back to traditional patterns and ways. Only a few were able to foster shared beliefs and faith in their novel approaches thus losing the support of parents and other important constituents.[1]

Given the experiences of Alternative Schools coupled with the spotty legacy of the non-stop parade of education reform, what can we rightfully expect or predict of the continuing experiences of charter schools and their creators? Do we at last have a stable alternative to traditional public schools? Or will Charter Schools join the carousel of promising new education ventures that endure for a limited time before scuttling in the wake of other efforts? Will a majority of the founders of Charter Schools have the stamina and leadership necessary to sustain the integrity of their initiative over time? Have Charter School leaders learned lessons that traditional school leaders should heed? What new challenges will leaders of Charter Schools face in the future? Are they ready for whatever lies ahead?

One of the persistent problems that traditional schools face is maintaining legitimacy. Unlike businesses, schools do not have a clear bottom line. Test scores sometimes offer an inkling of how well a school is performing. But too many other factors, such as social economic status (SES) and muddled results render standardized tests a relatively poor measure of student learning. Consequently, people look at other factors to determine how well a school is doing. Among these are a school's physical appearance, qualifications of faculty, or enthusiasm of students. Charter Schools have an advantage over regular public schools because students and teachers choose to attend. Choice implies that people, at some level, believe in the school and have faith in its ability to provide effective learning experiences. When, for a variety of reasons, belief and faith erode then people begin to question a school's ability to provide adequate learning. Questions often trigger doubt and doubt typically erodes faith and confidence.

We have followed a sample of Charters for several years. To what extent have they maintained their identity over time? Are the founders still involved in running the schools? Has the enterprise grown? What accounts for the school's success or lack thereof? What lessons does the school offer to others who wish to create a Charter? What role do Charter leaders play in a school? What can traditional schools learn from the experiences of Charter leaders? In the cases that follow we look at several schools at two points: early on in their development and as they have evolved over time. And at least in these case studies that follow, the schools were built to last and the leaders are still influencing their success.

Terrence E. Deal
Irving R. Melbo Professor
Rossier School of Education
University of Southern California

NOTE

1. Deal, Terrence E., and Nolan, Robert R. "Alternative Schools: A Conceptual Map." The School Review 87, no. 1 (November 1, 1978): 29–49.

Preface

Longtime friend and colleague, Terry Deal, has sketched a most appropriate context for this book—a historical portrait of the US public schools during which our current system was crafted and within which alternatives to that system also flowed and ebbed. From this perspective, charter schools are accurately characterized as among the more recent of a string of planned variations within our "one best system" of public schools. My happy task at this point is to dial up the figurative microscope and focus on the discrete but compelling story conveyed by this book's authors—the enduring relationship between charter school founders and their creations.

The DNA of school leadership is a proverbial double helix wherein the circumstances of the school inextricably influence, and are influenced by, the nature of its leaders. *Journeys of Charter School Creators: Leadership for the Long Haul* examines this interplay of charter school founders and the schools they created, but extends the interplay over time, almost two decades.

The central question that drove the authors of the original book, *Adventures of Charter School Creators: Leading from the Ground Up* (2004), on which this work was based was straightforward: what are the characteristics of people who elect first to imagine and then to create charter schools? After all, charter schools then were a new, hotly debated and largely untried school reform, joining a list of other controversial choice-based schemes. What kind of person would pursue this path to "school leadership"?

Although many volumes had been written on the roles of public school principal and private school headmaster, charters were sufficiently different, and the idea of creating a market-oriented public school out of whole cloth seemed like a radical departure from those roles. Were charter school founders simply slight variations on the historic theme of school leader, or, per their different backgrounds, interests, circumstances, and capabilities, did they really constitute a different kind of school leader? More pointedly, were these people behaving more like business entrepreneurs, fixated on starting a new enterprise of their own design, or were they more like traditional school leaders pursuing legacy roles as "principal teachers"?

The short answer is both. Although they had to address all of the classic concerns of today's school leader—instructional, curricular, pedagogical, student- and family-related, and so on—they also reflected characteristics of classic entrepreneurs, a seemingly very different category of leader that has also been extensively studied. More specifically, the charter school founders featured in this book exhibit classic entrepreneurial traits, such as tolerance for risk, desire for control, ambition, perseverance, and decisiveness. All traits in service of creating a new enterprise.

At the time, charter school legislation provided a new way to create new enterprises. When *Adventures* was written, the very idea of charter schools was embryonic—a public entity, such as a school district, awarding a charter to a private nonprofit group to create and operate a school based on an approved set of principles and practices. This covenant between public authorizers and private providers, enforceable through authorizer oversight and charter revocation/school closure, created an opportunity for charter school founders to transform their vision into "the schools they want," rather than settling for "the schools they have."

From zero charter schools about a quarter century ago, today there are more than seven thousand, together enrolling over three million students, and this growth shows no signs of abating. Today, new charter school creation is often driven by charter management organizations, and the start-up process has become widely known and shared through these and through many associations and businesses that specialize in helping to create, finance, supply, analyze, and market charter schools.

We know more about how the charter school movement has matured than we know about how charter school founders have matured. After creating charter schools, what do they do? What do they become? Why? Are they similar to other entrepreneurs who master the creation of the enterprise, but struggle in its operation and growth? Do they behave like principals in traditional public schools, often pursuing advancement through transfer to principal positions in other, often larger, schools or seeking positions in school district central offices?

The *Journeys* authors have pursued these questions of the maturing of charter school founders, and what they find seems at first counterintuitive, but upon reflection, entirely plausible. Seemingly idiosyncratic stories of individuals from widely differing backgrounds aggregate into a surprisingly coherent tapestry of "life after charter school creation."

In fundamental outlook, these individuals have not changed over time. They are known by others more for their creations, experience, enthusiasm, and beliefs than by their professional preparation and credentials. They were drawn from many different backgrounds, with one common thread running through their resumes—deep passion and experience working with and helping children and their families.

What was good for kids always came first, and the opportunity structure provided by charter schools provided them a viable means to that end. But to achieve that end, they had to journey into heretofore foreign fields including capital finance, business development, marketing, information systems, municipal politics, and public engagement, not to mention directing discrete initiatives such as securing facilities, growing organizational talent, ensuring cash flow, and meeting payrolls.

Although ideologically unbending ("all kids can learn given the right conditions"), they are exceptionally pragmatic, like Joe Maimone mortgaging his house to meet payrolls on the way to growing his school. These founders did what they felt they had to do in order for their schools to thrive and grow.

Perhaps the most striking feature that characterizes these maturing charter school founders is the enduring nature of their commitment to the schools they founded. While many have successfully transitioned school leadership to able successors, they have stayed involved, sometimes indirectly, with "their" schools.

Some have helped grow the single school into a cluster of schools. Others have found a role in assisting in the formation and growth of charter schools more generally. Some have found a way to extend their vision through leadership in charter school associations, as back-office service providers, and as policy advocates. Still others have helped to transport their original educational vision, for example, in project-based learning or arts-based instruction, to other charter schools.

Case after case, these charter school founders have stayed close to the schools they created and to the communities they served. What they tended not to do is transfer to another school or district and "move on" in a quest for professional advancement elsewhere. The opportunity structure provided by charter school legislation afforded them a precious (to them) chance to fulfill a dream of creating "their" school. It played into classic entrepreneurial traits. But, in creating their charter schools, they were also captured by them.

To see their creations evolve, grow, develop, and thrive is now a hard earned reward, not to be cast aside in a different educational setting for a "new" challenge. The schools they founded are integral parts of their DNA. If this is indicative of other charter school founders, it reveals a characteristic of school choice not well examined—the enriched school choice environment that charter schools have made available to potential educators, not just to students and to their families.

Guilbert C. Hentschke, Dean Emeritus
Rossier School of Education
University of Southern California

Introduction

How the Journey Began

In 2002 a team of researchers and practitioners all loosely or directly affili-
ated with the University of Southern California joined together to investigate
successful charter school leaders across the United States. Thirteen charter
leaders who were selected based on their remarkable efforts at creating and
sustaining a successful charter school (conversion or new school) participated
in the project. Each leader told the story of the inception of their school, the
mission, and the challenges of their start-up experiences. The resulting publication was the book *Adventures of Charter School Creators: Leading from
the Ground Up.*[1]

A new team of researchers and practitioners, including some from the
original project, has followed up with those successful charter school leaders
nearly two decades later. All of the charter schools featured in the original
Adventures book, with the exception of one, are flourishing today. Most of
the original leaders are still at it, too, albeit some are in different roles within
their organizations.

The original stories told by the school leaders are included in this sequel,
followed by interviews and updates on most of the original leaders as well as
some new leaders with whom they now partner. Three additional successful,
sustained charter leadership stories have been added to the work. All three
of these leaders have served for extended periods of time and all three have
maintained successful, growing charter schools over time.

These entrepreneurs, against the odds, have all poured their hearts, souls,
and a considerable portion of their adult lives into starting and sustaining
schools driven by a vision that they were determined to realize, of what might
be or, through their lenses, what could and should be a quality education for
children. The leaders ranged from an Episcopal priest starting a grassroots
effort in an impoverished part of Los Angeles County, to parents looking for

1

a rigorous classical curriculum in rural North Carolina, to a business owner with a passion for project-based learning in a small town in Minnesota. The list goes on.

The schools' missions and visions are as unique as the founders' backgrounds—from a small arts-based school in a quaint southern town to larger urban alternatives for failing students. One commonality is that each of these entrepreneurs saw and seized the opportunity that the charter school structure provided, an organizational framework with the freedom to create and develop an entirely new organization with a specific vision and mission that focused on the education of children without the typical limitations of big district bureaucracy and control.

This book tells the stories of their continued journeys. The project began three years ago when we tracked down the original founders. With IRB approval and consents in hand, we interviewed them to learn more about their adventures since their start-ups. All of the founders included in this follow-up book are still involved in their original schools in some way; however, each now shares leadership with a team of leaders.

In addition, the respective communities that these school leaders serve still support the original missions and the leaders keep the visions not only alive, but growing and expanding, providing even more opportunities for the organizations. This is not to say that the original leaders have any less of an impact than they had twenty years ago. Quite the contrary. They are all still vitally important to the sustained success of their schools.

While the original *Adventures* project allowed the charter leaders to tell their stories, for this project, we asked the leaders the following categories of questions. First, we asked them to reflect on their original adventures creating their charter schools and where they and their schools stand today in comparison. Next, we asked a series of questions to try and cull what characteristics or skills they attributed to their successes as leaders in their schools.

Finally, we asked the leaders about their initial preparation for their charter school journeys as well as how they would design programs to prepare future charter leaders. The follow-up chapters to each of the leaders' original stories include answers to these questions and pieces of the overall leader preparation program proposed in our concluding chapter.

As we interviewed our original leaders, it became apparent that the stories were no longer just about their leadership. They now included additional leaders that had emerged within the organizations as they evolved and grew. Thus additional interviews with these new leaders ensued. We also researched the histories of the schools since the original *Adventures* project, investigated available accountability measures, and scoured the internet for additional tidbits of information about their schools. This effort led to some follow-up interviews, including some with community members, all of which was validating.

The stories of their *Journeys* are not just about the leaders themselves, but about the communities that have formed and thrived around the original vision and beliefs concerning the way education should and could look for children. They are about the many individuals coming together to take action on those beliefs. We were reminded of Roland Barth's quote made before the first state charter legislation ever passed, "A definition of leadership that I like is 'making happen what you believe in.'"[2] These charter leaders unquestionably have done just that.

We also coded the transcripts of our interviews with the leaders and interviews with others about the leaders, and were able to document sixty-eight characteristics, traits, and skills of these educational leaders who had opened and achieved sustained success in charter schools across the country. We grouped those skills and traits into five major themes. All of the leaders could be characterized by 1) A laser focus on quality results; 2) Strong interpersonal skills (people skills with a focus on relationship building); 3) A strong work ethic (paired with humility); 4) A growth mind-set (optimistic with problems seen as opportunities); and lastly, a batch of unique leadership skills and traits based on prior experiences were lumped into category five, Other (two of the leaders were former military workers, one was a priest, several had prior business experience and expertise).

Their combined stories showed evidence of these themes, their skills, and characteristics, and how they parlayed their strengths and abilities to approach and overcome challenges and sustain success. Each leader also shared the belief that while they held talents in some specific areas, they needed to build a reliable, strong team to complement their strengths, and they needed and readily used some form of distributive leadership (and were able to build the relationships to accomplish this).

These themes would likely not be a surprise to a scholar of leadership theory. Plenty of leadership literature points to the need for strong people skills, a focus on quality, believing in one's effort and working one's tail off to achieve success. However, two additional similarities across the stories were more noteworthy.

First, the level of commitment of these leaders to a specific population of students was unusual. While many school leadership preparation programs ready leaders for any multitude of schools or district office positions, we know of none that ask a leader to select one community of kids that need help and devote a quarter of a century of their lives toward that effort. The steadfastness of this group of leaders resembled more missionary work than school work and the commitment more closely resembled a marriage than a job. They all went to literally any degree necessary to achieve success for their communities of learners. They all mentioned a willingness to roll up their sleeves and get done whatever had to get done from mopping floors and scrubbing toilets to mortgaging their own homes to take out loans for construction projects for the schools. (We felt that this extended beyond simply a "strong work ethic.")

As you will find in these stories, these leaders refused to accept failure or in most cases, take "no" for an answer. Instead, they each saw closed doors or challenges as opportunities for creative thinking and for potentially building new relationships. They relished problem-solving and we did not hear a single challenge posed as a complaint, but as opportunities to think anew or differently about possible solutions.

This brings us to our second and perhaps more interesting finding. While these leaders were able to build strong and broad teams to support their efforts, they were viewed nonetheless as "the leader" of their organizations and their influence was apparent in all aspects of the journey by all stakeholders, including their instructional leaders that emerged along their journeys.

We learned this through additional interviews, not necessarily through the leaders themselves, who were especially humble in sharing their leadership styles and skills. Interestingly, it was the freedom provided by the charter school opportunity itself that, in retrospect, seemed to serve as an opportunity structure through which these leaders could make their influence felt much more deeply, broadly and powerfully and they made their dreams reality. Leaders in charter schools clearly matter—perhaps more so than in traditional public schools.

While many, if not most, are now of retirement age, all of the original charter leaders are still involved in their schools. Some of the leaders continue to serve on their charter school boards, others have moved to more of a consulting role, and some still remain very active in the day-to-day operations of the schools. All of the original leaders exhibited an ability to develop a team of leaders over time to cultivate a deep, connected community that to this day maintains the foundation of support for each school.

Those original entrepreneurs who were strong in management, partnered with instructional leaders, and each founder balanced his or her strengths by partnering with others who complemented them. In virtually every case, the instructional leaders were "in on the ground floor" in some way in the original creation of the charter. Many of them had started as teachers in the schools. The longtime leader of the Arts-Based School, Robin Hollis, was actually a parent the first year the school opened, and has served as its leader ever since taking over in year two.

THE JOURNEYS CONTINUE

In this book, each original *Adventures* chapter is immediately followed in order by its updated chapter about the same school and leader. The updates are about the leaders, albeit not *by* the leaders, and so, we hope, offer additional insights into their successful, sustained leadership for the long haul. In each case, the original chapter authors assisted with their follow-up stories. The schools are grouped by some noted similarities and progress in order to show expansion and variety of approaches.

The two opening school stories were founded with project-based, hands-on curriculum designs as their mission. The first of these, Minnesota New Country School, began as a high school while the second, Odyssey Charter School, began as a K–8 school. Odyssey has since expanded to add a second school which also includes younger children, while New Country has added lower grades and is now a K–12 institution. These two applied-learning school approaches are followed by the story of an arts-based charter and then a school that emerged from a "mass in the grass" to a multifaceted organization which educates over 3,600 students on multiple campuses as well as encompassing programs that educate parents and community members. The variety of schools and leaders is entertaining if not exhilarating.

The final three stories of the book include the adventures of three additional charter school leaders who were not part of the original 2004 *Adventures* journey. All three of these schools were created by their leaders within one state (North Carolina) and all provide additional examples of sustained, successful charter school leadership for the long haul.

PREPARING FUTURE LEADERS

In conclusion, we documented the voices of all of these charter leaders as they chimed in regarding their advisement on preparation programs for the type of entrepreneurial school leadership that opening a charter school requires. There was a unanimous request for a greater emphasis on teaching more business-related skills in any preparation programs.

The business aspects of running charter schools, negotiating and entering into contracts, preparing budgets, project management, and so on, these skills were unanimously found to be lacking in all of their programs, traditional or nontraditional. They all wished they had learned more about the finance of starting schools and those with strong business backgrounds all relied heavily on that knowledge and experience, reporting that it was, hands down, their most important training for their positions.

They also relied on instructional leadership, often provided by the teachers or others within the schools. However, they noted that they had to have the people skills to find, keep, and cultivate those instructional leaders wherever they found them. As they helped engage and grow the skills of other leadership team members, it was not in an effort to replace themselves. While many of today's school leadership programs typically teach candidates to build leadership capacity within an organization, which all of these charter leaders did, in the event that they moved on, the charter leaders did not build it to prepare for their own exit to the next school or the next job. They stayed. And all of their "next" projects revolved around their original charter school effort, sometimes combined with furthering the charter school cause.

Finally, each piece of wisdom shared by these leaders reminded us of the importance of perseverance and diligence as they noted that a true leader leads by example, no job is beneath or above him or her, and future leaders must not be afraid of tackling problems and engaging in creative thinking to design and make happen the ideal learning environments for all children to which they aspire.

NOTES

1. Terrence E. Deal, Guilbert C. Hentschke, Kendra Kecker, Christopher Lund, Scot Oschman and Rebecca Shore *Adventures Of Charter School Creators: Leading From the Ground Up* (Lanham, MD: Scarecrow Education, 2004).

2. Roland S. Barth, "A Personal Vision of a Good School," *Phi Delta Kappan* 71, no. 7 (1990): 512–16.

Chapter 1

Owning Wobegon

DOUG THOMAS, MINNESOTA
NEW COUNTRY SCHOOL

Doug Thomas was director of the Gates-EdVisions Project and president of EdVisions, Inc, the nonprofit corporation hosting the effort funded by the Bill and Melinda Gates Foundation to replicate the learning model of the New Country School and the teacher-owner model of EdVisions Cooperative. Thomas was the University of Minnesota's Center for School Change outreach coordinator for southern Minnesota for ten years, working to create new kinds of public schools in rural communities. He served four terms on the Le Sueur-Henderson Board of Education and six years on the board of the South Central Minnesota Service Cooperative. He has five years of teaching experience in rural towns and for ten years was a small-business owner. His special areas of interest are rural community development, secondary education reform, and leadership for educational change.

It's now been over ten years since the first planners met to discuss the creation of what was to become one of the most unusual and celebrated charter schools in America. The New Country School planning process began in the halls and basement of the 1,900 portion of the old Henderson High School, located approximately 60 miles southwest of Minneapolis, a farm country along the Minnesota River Valley. A couple of teachers, myself, and a few local business people first met in the teachers' work room to sketch out a plan for a new kind of computer-infused high school. That first meeting was invaded by the local superintendent who sternly warned the group, "You had better not be talking about a charter school." He subsequently banned the group from meeting on school grounds.

"The . . . superintendent . . . warned . . . 'You had better not be talking about a charter school.' He subsequently banned the group from meeting on school grounds."

So it was in bars and coffee shops for the next eighteen months that this group of entrepreneurs and school reformers pursued their dream. I was the convener of sorts. I was two years into a position at the Center for School Change at the Humphrey Institute for Public Affairs at the University of Minnesota and knew a little about the landmark charter law Minnesota had passed the year before. I also had access to the best minds and activists around the school reform work of the early 1990s: Joe Nathan, Ted Kolderie, Wayne Jennings, Ted Sizer, and others. My job was to help create new kinds of public school, schools-within-schools, magnet schools, and charter schools if possible. Thus, it was not so accidental that I came to be involved in the making of a school.

What was more accidental was the place where that school began. Most people find it highly unlikely that such a school would be found in the heart of rural Minnesota, where the kids are all "above average." I had been on the local school board for about five years in 1992 and was committed to making high school more interesting and friendly. My own experience as a teacher, relatively short at four years, was one of boredom and frustration. My own small high school education, in Henderson, was one of tremendous personalization and nonstop activity, total immersion in sports, drama, music, community service, and academics (when we could fit them in). I knew school could be more than regimentation, rules, and elitism. The local school had consolidated with the bigger neighbor, taking the local kids out of their community and giving them less opportunity to participate in the kinds of activities that develop true active citizenship and leadership. What tipped the scales for me was a survey done in the local high school in which 70 percent of the students indicated their school "was not a good place to be." How could we stand for that many students being unsatisfied? It had to affect the entire culture of the school and community.

"My own experience as a teacher...was one of boredom and frustration... What tipped the scales for me was...70 percent of the students indicated their school 'was not a good place to be.'"

So I began to recruit and we began to meet. I recruited teachers, ex-teachers, board members, former board members, mentor teachers from Minnesota State University-Mankato, and business people who were both entrepreneurs and reformers. We even got a few students to join us. We met every couple of weeks for a year before we let our plans be known.

Our premise was to take the typical high school and look at each major design feature and decide whether that piece made sense in terms of what it did for the students. At the end of the year, we had nothing left that looked like a traditional high school: no classes, no grades, no bells, no principal, a weeklong break every six weeks, personal work stations, and a computer for every student, public presentation of student work, and a building that would look more like a busy office. And it would be small, no more than 150 students.

When the news of the new school came out, some were shocked and insulted, others inquisitive and interested. The school board was not impressed and turned down the request for sponsorship 6-0 (I had to abstain). We were disheartened but immediately turned our attention to a neighboring district, which subsequently refused to take a vote for not wanting to appear anti-reform. Little consolation for us. But Le Sueur-Henderson's new super-intendent, Dr. Harold Laron, came back to us and asked if we would like to participate in a districtwide, strategic planning process to take place in the summer of 1993. We agreed, and the resulting plan called for a new kind of high school model. Later that fall, the board unanimously voted to sponsor the Minnesota New Country School.

At that point, the real planning began. We had less than a year to recruit students and teachers, find a place to locate, and develop a program that no one in the country had yet to try. We had only our good intentions and advice from folks like Joe Nathan and Wayne Jennings, who had started the St. Paul Open School twenty years before. We began meeting weekly, and with no start-up funds and only our good name and intuition, we created a school from scratch.

We had one big political hurdle to overcome yet. Three months after our sponsorship, we were ready to take the contract back to the board. In many ways this was more crucial than sponsorship because it committed the district to three years of experimenting with an autonomous, new, and different kind of public school arrangement. We were asking the district, in Ted Kolkerie's words, "To trust someone other than the typical district and its employees to provide the service of public education." It was a very intense couple of weeks. The opposition and the press wanted all the answers now. They wanted to know where we would locate, how students would be bused, and how many students from the district would attend. We didn't have many of the answers. The board took testimony for six and a half hours, mostly from current high school teachers opposing the reform ideas and the need for such a school. We got a few experts to come in and support our ideas but mostly relied on our ability to convince people of our sincerity and the growing need to change high schools.

"This is not your money. This is not our money. This money belongs to parents and their children, and if 60 or 70 of them choose to spend it differently, I can't stand in their way."

The stars must have been aligned the following week when the board voted 5-1 to approve the contract. The key point in the process was when the board chair, Virginia Miller, spoke eloquently about the reality of school choice coming to a small Minnesota school district. She looked at the crowd that had gathered, many of them opposing teachers, and said, "This is not your money. This is not our money. This money belongs to parents and their children, and if 60 or 70 of them choose to spend it differently, I can't stand in their way." The superintendent nodded in agreement and the contract vote was approved. Years later, I still think about that moment and how important that statement has become and how charged the question of public school choice remains. It seems never about doing the right thing but about money. We wouldn't create big boxes with 2,000 students if it wasn't about the money.

"Ted Kolderie . . . asked if we'd be interested in creating a school that had no employees. . . . The idea was for a teacher professional practice, legally organized as a cooperative,...[that would] own the instructional service at the school."

The rest is history. Well, not exactly. Charter schools are always evolving. They never take a break from change or controversy. We set about preparing for our opening in Fall 1994. We found a couple of empty storefronts in downtown Le Sueur and remodeled up to the opening day. Parents and potential students helped out immensely those first few months prior to and after opening. I still can't believe they were so patient and trusting that first year. The program was totally unknown and untried. The buildings were less than adequate, and some of the first students were troubled, having come from a variety of school districts (this seemed to be their latest stop). The original teachers (Ron Newell, Nancy Miller, Kim Borwege, and John Brosnan), two who came from the traditional school, one a local techie, and one a MSU mentor with twenty-five years of experience, were motivated but unsure. I think what saved us that first year was that the planners were there almost daily, trying to help the teachers pragmatically and with the big picture. We kept reminding them at our weekly meetings that they were doing groundbreaking work and others would be looking at their success or failure. Admittedly, we put pressure on them they probably didn't need.

Shortly after our initial contract approval, we put another twist on this story. Ted Kolderie approached us with a question and an idea. He asked if we'd be interested in creating a school that had no employees. As you can imagine, we were puzzled but very intrigued. I'd always been interested in alternative business practices. The idea was for a teacher professional practice, legally organized as a cooperative, to own the instructional service at the school. In other words, a cooperative made up of teachers and others would contract for the learning program at the school. The staff would receive a lump-sum amount of money (for compensation, staff development, etc.) and then decide among themselves how it would be spent, thus eliminating the board from the tedious work of negotiating every person's worth and pay. The group was not all that excited about the idea, especially since Minnesota charter were governed by a teacher majority board already. After several hours of discussing and selling the idea, I was able to convince everyone it was worth a try. If we didn't make history with our unique school design, we were certainly going to with the teacher ownership and professionalism model.

I and others were especially excited about EdVisions Cooperative because the group decided to allow for "at large" membership. This allowed those of us who had been part of the planning team to remain involved at the learning program level. The initial group included about fourteen members, including Dr. Larson, the superintendent. Essentially, we directed the program those first years of the school. Today, EdVisions Cooperative has grown to include 9 schools, 125 teachers, a dozen at-large members, a small group of consulting members, and a nonprofit arm that has set about creating more New Country-like schools. A recently published book about the professional practice idea, *Teachers As Owners*, is available through Scarecrow Press.

The New Country School itself has evolved. Although still holding true to its original premise, it has developed a bit more structured, but very respected, project-based learning model. The school still has no courses or bells and no formal principal. Still run by the teachers, it is now located on Main Street in Henderson in a new facility that was designed to mirror the unique learning program. There are the high-tech personal work stations for each student, lots of room for project work, a science lab and media resource center, and a stage area for public presentation of student work, plays, and community events. The building project in 1998 was a unique partnership between a local development group, the City of Henderson, the US Department of Agriculture Rural Development, and a local bank. The New Country School has become an economic development success story. It attracts over 500 visitors from around the world each year, and the cooperative has created several jobs for this small community of 1,000 residents.

The school has had a measure of success beyond the novelty and publicity, as well. Standardized and other measures are positive, and student and parent satisfaction is always tremendous. The combination of technology and self-directed earning is very popular and works with all ability levels. The staff at New Country has spent considerable time over the years improving the learning process and fine-tuning the project system, weaving in the state performance standards, making sure the basic skills are attained, and preparing young people for the world of work and postsecondary school. About 70 percent of New Country's graduates go on to further schooling. Nearly all the students attend some college while in high school through Minnesota's postsecondary enrollment program.

"Some still think the school is either for 'tech-heads' or at-risk students."

Reaction to the school has been mixed over the years. I think generally the public has accepted the idea that we need a variety of schools to serve students' needs. Many still don't understand or appreciate the differences in our school. They see on the surface that the school doesn't have its own sports teams (they have a pairing arrangement with the district). Some still think the school is either for "tech-heads" or at-risk students. The building is getting more and more community use, so that tends to break down the barriers to a certain extent.

After eight years, there are no original board members left on the district board, and Superintendent Larson has retired. The former high school principal is now the superintendent and is generally supportive. The various board members have been helpful over the years, especially when the different academic program is explained and they get firsthand knowledge of how it works well for students. They appreciate, too, the teacher cooperative model, especially when they see how many of their own issues are tied to collective bargaining and union versus management politics. Those difficulties are virtually nonexistent in the cooperative model or are internal to the cooperative group.

Some of the original planners are still present but working in different capacities. Ron Newell is the learning programs director for the Gates-EdVisions Project of EdVisions, Inc., the nonprofit arm of the cooperative. He recently authored a book about project-based learning, *A Passion for Learning* (Scarecrow Press). The Gates-EdVisions Project is a multimillion-dollar replication project funded by the Bill and Melinda Gates Foundation. I am now the president of EdVisions, Inc. (nonprofit), and director of the Gates-EdVisions Project, after spending ten years with the Center for School Change. Nancy Miller returned to the local high school to retire and take advantage of a lucrative severance package. Kim Borwege spent seven years with new Country until accepting a position in the district where she lived. John Brosnan returned to the private technology company he had been employed by before teaching at New Country. Two of the original planners, Dee Thomas and Dena Link, are now teacher/advisors at the school. Dee Thomas is a member of the Minnesota State Board of Teaching and president of the Minnesota Associate of Charter Schools. Dean Lind and Ron Newell are active members of the board of directors of EdVisions Cooperative. Together, we all keep the fire burning.

"If a group of naïve country [educators] in a typical school district can do this, anybody can."

The Gates-EdVisions Project is charged with creating fifteen new schools like New Country School and ten new teacher-owner models like EdVisions Cooperative. We now have a small staff, located in downtown Henderson, and have nine new schools up and running in Minnesota and Wisconsin and are working on a national scale-up effort. It is truly a dream come true for many of us who started the New Country School. Our mission was to create a great, small, innovative school and to change the world of high school education. We often joke about being "farm kids with attitude" and trying to "save the world." The truth is that the charter venture is hard, sometimes scary work. If you don't have a passion to make things better for kids and adults, you tend to run out of energy or lose interest in the fight. As Joe Nathan reminded me so often at the Center for School Change, "This is a marathon, not a sprint."

My personal reflection is quite positive. I've heard all the clichés about small groups doing great things. Now I've seen it happen and know it can happen over and over again across this country. If a group of naïve country kids in a typical school district can do this, anybody can. The heart and soul of public education is the entrepreneurial spirit that comes from parents, educators, and students joining together to create something wonderful. I can't help but think this is the beginning of the reindependence of public education, this infusion of spirit that has often been zapped by the bureaucracy.

Leadership is all about ideas and people. It's the infusion of ideas into people's hearts and minds to help them do something extraordinary. I'm certain there will be a new culture created around charter schools, one with a new freedom and motivation to say "we can" when dreaming about what might happen for kids. We often say this is "missionary work," converting one soul at a time. For me, the past ten years have been just that, working with one person or a small group to help them realize the possibilities of acting on their dreams.

Chapter 2

Teacher-Owned, Student-Driven

Minnesota New Country School (MNCS) located in Henderson, Minnesota, is far from a traditional school and very different than many other charter schools. MNCS is in tune with some of what Albert Shanker, the former president of the American Federation of Teachers, may have had in mind.

When the concept of charter schools was introduced by Shanker, in a 1988 address to the profession, "innovative," "student-centered," and "parent/teacher-lead" were descriptors often used. Shanker had just returned from a trip to Cologne, Germany, where he visited some interesting public schools blazing new territory. At one of the German schools, teams of teachers had considerable authority regarding how the school was run, how to teach, and even how to structure the grade levels. Many of them stayed with their students over six years, moving up a grade as the students progressed.

"When the concept of charter schools was introduced . . . "innovative," "student-centered," and "parent/teacher-lead" were descriptors often used."

Charter schools were proposed by Shanker and others to be unique organizations designed to meet the needs of a small population of students and their families who need/want something different than the traditional public school. Doug Thomas and EdVisions Schools, who helped start Minnesota New Country School, believed MNCS may have been the type of school Shanker had in mind. MNCS definitely embodies the innovative, parent/teacher-lead, student-centered vision of the original charter school focus.

Nestled in a small town in Minnesota, New Country School continues to serve a small population of high school students and has since its opening added elementary school students. The original charter called for a project-based high school to serve approximately 120 students in grades 7 through 12. The founders were insistent that this wasn't going to become the "big-box" standardized high school of the day. It would be a place where teachers knew their students well!

Based on community interest, in 2013 an equally innovative, child-centered elementary school with nearly 100 K–6 students was added to the secondary school. The two campuses now serve more than 200 students in grades K–12. Some students travel a substantial distance from thirteen surrounding communities within a 45-mile radius to attend this little gem. Run by teachers who carry a variety of roles, MNCS has influenced not only its students and families but also a host of guests who visit from around the country to learn about the unique program.

"The founders were insistent that this wasn't going to become the 'big-box' standardized high school of the day. It would be a place where teachers knew their students well!"

What's still so unique about MNCS? Two teacher advisors, Aaron Grimm and Paul Jaegar, shared why MNCS is distinctive. Two components that make this school different are: 1) its teacher-owned cooperative and 2) the student-driven, project-based approach to learning.

The teacher-owned cooperative is a distributive, teacher-leader model of daily governance in which the teachers are owners, not employees. Maintaining the culture and integrity of the school are essential elements closely monitored by lead teachers; however, all school decisions are made through teacher consensus. All teachers serve on site-based management teams focused on areas such as personnel, curriculum, community involvement, special education, transportation-building-grounds, technology, finance, marketing, and senior presentation. Time and energy are allocated to teacher planning and evaluation.

While EdVisions Cooperative (MNCS's formal employer who contracts their services) and the small school board provide oversight via human resources, payroll, and benefits, the teachers collaborate to insure compliance and innovation are both achieved.

"As teacher owners, we sink or swim together. The stakes are high and gone are the traditional scapegoats: the incompetent administrator, the madcap superintendent, the unhinged department chair."

A perfect example of this collaborative, teacher-led effort has been deemed noteworthy to be shared on the US Department of Education website.[1] When faced with a financial situation where the budget needed to be reduced, instead of cutting an aide's position, the staff decided to each accept a $2,500 pay cut to fund the aide so they would not lose the position. The decision was reached through consensus. Paul Jaeger, a high school advisor, shared his thoughts on the benefits of the teacher-owned school configuration:

> As teacher owners, we sink or swim together. The stakes are high and gone are the traditional scapegoats: the incompetent administrator, the madcap superintendent, the unhinged department chair. At MNCS, the strength of our community (colleagues, students, parents, community members) is positively dependent on our willingness to look to one another when the going gets tough to find the best way to do right by our kids.

"'Doing right by kids' is a phrase that runs through MNCS's belief system."

While the teachers work collaboratively to run the organization, the students, with guidance from their advisors and teachers, determine their own learning journey and destiny. New Country inspires innovation through this personalized, student-led, project-based approach. While the charter currently operates on two sites, the elementary site for grades K–6, and the high school site for grades 7–12, MNCS treats the two campuses as one community of learners, K–12.

Students are viewed as the builders and keepers of school culture. This prompts the policy of upper-level students mentoring the younger students. The students naturally develop leadership roles. The goal is for graduating seniors to know how to learn anything they want to learn and to be able to execute on projects that are important to them. The K–12 experience gives them the time to develop the skills and abilities to reach that goal.

At the elementary level, basic skills such as math, reading, and writing are taught; however, additional curricular areas set this school apart from other local elementary schools. There is a focus on environmental experiential learning, an introduction to project-based learning, the responsive classroom approach, character education, and infused technology.

Another unique feature of this elementary school is the multiage classrooms. Kindergarten is the only single grade classroom. Each promotion or placement decision is purposeful with a focus more on the student rather than the grade-level framework used at most schools; the multiage classrooms are designed to help students understand that learning is not based on grade levels.

In the upper elementary levels, projects begin to be more student-directed with guidance from advisors. As the students move into the higher grades (7–12), the curriculum becomes even more student-led. At this stage, some students may need help framing an idea they have, creating a plan of action for a project, or getting unstuck on a difficult phase of a project. The job of the advisor is to understand the students in their advisory group, listen to each student with care, and help them get the support they need. The school handbook outlines the policies and structure of the students' progression through self-directed, project-based learning.

The high school has been described as the "modern version of a one-room schoolhouse" in a large open space surrounded by a science lab, a library, art and recording studios, and a shop. Workstations complete with computers are available for students to work independently or collaboratively. A stage, a dual-purpose conference and classroom space created from a grain silo, and common tables for group work, lunch, and meeting space are centrally located in the building. There are no bells, class periods, grades, or homework.

"The high school has been described as the "modern version of a one-room schoolhouse" in a large open space surrounded by a science lab, a library, art and recording studios, and a shop."

The entire academic program at the high school level is student-centered and project-based. Jaeger explained that teacher time is spent on getting to know the students and their interests to make learning interesting and motivating for them. Part of his job is to connect students with the experts and resources to extend their learning. Teachers are learning alongside their students. Jaeger said,

Developing quality relationships with students is critical in any educational setting and paramount in a learner-centered environment. Without positive and professional relationships in place, nothing else matters. Advisors at MNCS are learners first and teachers second. The most crucial subject for us to learn about and understand is our students. What do they care about? How do they motivate themselves to get stuff done? If they need help, do they know how to ask for it?

Fortunately, our learner-centered environment affords us with opportunities to get to know our students and grow our community. We are not pouring energy into designing curriculum; we are guiding students through their project work. We do not spend precious time grading student work (*we do not have grades); we ascribe worth to the things they are doing well and, if given permission, offer them growth challenges in areas they can improve.

As an advisor at MNCS, one job I have is to help my advisees find their Yoda(s)—the people who can teach them the things they want to know. One of the great freedoms we all have is being able to decide who our teachers are. This might be an actual teacher, but for many, it is someone else entirely: a YouTuber, a blogger, a friend, a community elder. For instance, one of the students I am lucky to work with has an abiding interest in green architecture. I am out of my depth in that particular field, but one of our community members has been a practicing architect for two decades. Putting students in touch with the right teacher(s) is an important part of our work at MNCS. Of greater import, in finding the right teachers, students are learning how to learn what they want to learn.

The lessons shared by the advisors go beyond teaching curriculum; they strive to facilitate learning that empowers students to be lifelong learners. While no mention of Ted Sizer's Coalition of Essential School Principles were specially mentioned, all were present at MNCS.

"In a culture that does not allow for failure, there will be little innovation."

It isn't surprising that the recent standardization movement in the United States is a real dilemma for schools like MNCS. Doug Thomas, one of the original founders and a true proponent of the EdVisions School's philosophy based on progressive student-led, project-based education, shared his views on the biggest obstacle to innovation:

> The biggest demand on charter school leaders over the past dozen years is the standardization vs. innovation dilemma. . . . Charter schools were meant to infuse innovation into a stagnant institution, not necessarily by creating competition but by being allowed to try different approaches with some failing along the way. In a culture that does not allow for failure, there will be little innovation. Few charter schools have truly been allowed to innovate. The standards movement drags them back to the conventional. This has put true leadership to the test, frustrating most intended transformational leaders.

While MNCS follows the regulations and accountability measures demanded of them, they focus on motivating students to learn through project-based learning opportunities. Teaching to specific standards that may be tested on a standardized test is not part of the makeup of MNCS.

Thomas shared his thoughts on standards, "Standard outcomes! If you keep doing the same thing you will keep getting the same outdated, irrelevant outcomes." Achievement scores in Math and Reading fell below the state's overall scores according to the 2016–2017 Minnesota Department of Education. While MNCS assures that the students will meet the state standards by passing the Minnesota Basic Skills Test, teachers assert that college entry rates and report card scores don't paint the entire picture. Thomas concludes, "But foremost is the ability to innovate so that young people are motivated to learn. That will take both formal and out-of-the-box training, thinking and experimenting and most important, communicating with parents, students and teachers."

At MNCS students develop skills to problem solve, communicate, and manage; moreover, they learn to become responsible for their lifelong learning. MNCS prepares its students to be college and career ready, based on its students' interests, not on the standards set by the state. It's works for them and the families they serve.

"MNCS prepares its students to be college and career ready, based on its students' interests, not on the standards set by the state. It's works for them and the families they serve."

While the size of New Country has remained small to maintain personalized instruction, the number of charter schools assisted by EdVisions Schools has grown significantly. After visiting MNCS, representatives from the Bill and Melinda Gates Foundation, in an effort to replicate the school, awarded a grant of $4.3 million dollars to start fifteen schools in Minnesota and Wisconsin.

A second grant of $4.5 million was awarded to spread the replication effort nationwide. Since that time, EdVisions Schools helped create over forty schools in thirteen states and has been instrumental in the start-up of guiding over 200 schools throughout the United States. EdVisions' mission remains the same, "to support new school development and the transformation of existing schools that wish to create more personalized, engaging learning through meaningful and relevant, student-centered project based learning and teacher empowerment."

Doug Thomas, one of the founders of MNCS and EdVisions Schools, is now retired but continues to serve on the board of EdVisions. Thomas views himself as a "connector." He was able to bring the right people together when it was important and reach out to a wider circle of folks who could help realize the vision of Minnesota New Country School and the many schools modeled after it.

"There were lots of awards and events over the years but our real accomplishment was getting the innovation to stick during a time of standardization and re-trenching."

After nearly twenty-five years since the formation of EdVisions Schools and MNCS, Thomas shared his thoughts on what has been accomplished by this nonprofit educational development organization and its first innovative teacher-owned, student-centered, project-based school:

I would say the connection to policy folks and the resulting state policy changes were a critical outcome for us in that many of the ideas or innovations were put in place because of the work of the Minnesota New Country School and EdVisions. This was a true example of "connecting" with the right people and staying on task as we pushed for fundamental changes in education. For a non-graded, non-course based, project learning high school to have gained the attention of legislators and stayed in the forefront for almost twenty years, has been a real accomplishment. There were lots of awards and events over the years but our real accomplishment was getting the innovation to stick during a time of standardization and re-trenching.

Thomas reminded us earlier, that if a school like MNCS can be successful in a small town in Minnesota, it can be done anywhere. A combination of passion, entrepreneurial spirit, and hard work paired with a strong team of dedicated individuals can lead to more schools that "Do right by kids!"

NOTE

1. US Department of Education. Retrieved May 23, 2018. https://www2.ed.gov/admins/comm/choice/charterhs/report_pg18.html.

Chapter 3

Guarding the Mission

KATHLEEN O'SULLIVAN, ODYSSEY
CHARTER SCHOOL

Odyssey Charter School, an independent public school chartered by the Los Angeles County Board of Education, is located in Pasadena and serves a diverse community of 240 K–8 students who learn best by doing. Kathleen O'Sullivan, the founder and a member of the governing board, piloted Odyssey through its first years of operation as the executive director and has worked with a multitude of organizations—federal, state, local, and private— during the past six years to bring her dream to a working reality. O'Sullivan is a highly skilled communicator, trainer, and facilitator who identifies a problem, works to solve it, and moves on to the next challenge. Over the past ten years, she has developed expertise in workforce preparation, particularly with at-risk youth. She has over twenty-five years of business experience in public, private, and nonprofit settings in the areas of recruitment, employee development, marketing and sales, program development, fund raising, and grant writing, and she draws on her professional and personal experiences as a student, wife, mother, foster parent, and grandparent to create and sustain the vision of Odyssey. O'Sullivan and her husband, Michael, an architect, live in South Pasadena.

Odyssey Charter School is located in Pasadena, California. At the outset of our third year of operation, I am proud to say Odyssey's success is a result of sometimes heroic efforts by many, while weathering the challenges and opportunities that await any new and innovative venture, admittedly by just hanging on one minute longer in many cases.

To understand Odyssey's vision is to understand how and why it was birthed. Unlike many charter school developers, my background is not that of a formal educator, nor did I intend to reform education from the perspective of academia. On the contrary, my motivation for venturing into this unchartered territory was driven by a passion that grew out of my twenty-five years of experience in the corporate, nonprofit, and public sectors, working for others and for myself, much of which involved training and development. By nature, I am an entrepreneur. I delight in finding innovative solutions that will make a difference, then empowering others to take ownership and grow the vision and the capacity for fulfilling it. Over the years, my work has resulted in successful and innovative programs that have been able to stand on their own as I have moved on.

As a result of my experience and observations in the workplace, and perhaps a bit of providence, I made a decision about ten years ago to take my career in a new direction. I became immersed in the arena of workforce preparation and workforce development. I was determined to find creative ways to help at-risk youth prepare themselves for the world of work, and to assist adults who were trying to get off welfare and into the work place. This was my most challenging and rewarding work. Most discouraging was my work with experienced and successful individuals who were suddenly and unexpectedly facing a career transition because their jobs no longer existed.

I found common ground among all these individuals, even though they seemingly had little in common. Regardless of their level of education, training, or experience, these individuals were rarely equipped with the skills that would help them transfer whatever knowledge and skills they had from one environment to another, whether it was from one subject to another in school, from school to the community, or from one job to another in the workplace. All had acquired knowledge but were ill equipped to apply that knowledge in a meaning way, or transfer that knowledge into another context.

In addition, many of these individuals were lacking the all-important "soft skills" needed to become responsible citizens and successful in the workplace—skills that help individuals succeed, whether they are the janitor or the CEO, inexperienced or experienced, at-risk or highly educated. They include such things as personal qualities, critical thinking skills, people skills, the ability to manage information and resources effectively, and an understanding of how systems work. These are all highly valued in the workplace, as well as essential to relationships, and yet they are given little attention in our educational system. Not surprisingly, those who seem naturally to possess these soft skills often succeed in spite of their education, training, or previous experience. Those who are lacking in these soft skills often fail, even if they are highly educated and well trained in job-specific skills.

This may account for why so many young adults find entry into the "real world" so difficult, and why many experienced and respected professionals are at a total loss when faced with having to make a shift into a new career. Schools today are focused, if not obsessed, with measuring how much knowledge has been gained, often at the expense of helping students learn how to learn and to discern when it might be appropriate to unlearn something. With such a narrow focus, we undermine our ability to create lifelong learners and skillful thinkers. I became more and more convinced that we must figure out a way for our educational system, from kindergarten on up, to incorporate opportunities to develop these soft skills in a purposeful manner.

"Sadly, for my children and many others (including myself), school became boring, uninspiring, and all about compliance."

My direct experience with the educational system has been both as a student and as a parent. I have been blessed with children (natural, foster, and adopted) who are bright, naturally precocious, curious, and very active. Like many children, growing up they were doers, and "why" seemed their favorite word. I'm sure my parents would voice the same about me, too. For children who continually challenge every assumption possible, school is rarely a safe, nurturing place. Worse, all too often these students are misunderstood and even mislabeled. They are no small challenge for the parent or for the traditional school system, public and private alike. Sadly, for my children and many others (including myself), school became boring, uninspiring, and all about compliance.

There was one exception for me as a student that was to forever change my view of education. At the age of 16, I had the opportunity and privilege of performing with *Up With People* and becoming a student in their newly formed high school. I joined 100 students from around the world in the adventure of a lifetime. We traveled full-time performing an inspiring two-hour musical wherever we went. Sixteen teachers traveled with us, mostly by bus, sometimes by train. The towns we visited throughout North America and the families and fellow students we stayed with during that year became our classroom. It challenged everything I knew about education and about people. All of us struggled for at least three months to figure out how to function in this classroom without walls, with the opportunity and responsibility of designing our own learning projects. I stayed on an extra year after graduation to do advanced public relations. It called upon every possible resource I had, and then some. It provided advanced training in how to live and work with people who are different from me, and how not to give in to uncertainty and adversity, something I would call upon throughout my life. It was terrifying, enlightening, and extremely rewarding. I wouldn't trade those experiences for anything!

The idea to create Odyssey Charter School was first conceived in the spring of 1998. I had started a private consulting business, Purposeful Training Systems, LLC, in the beginning of 1997 and had just completed writing *Ready for Success*™, a workforce preparation curriculum designed for at-risk students and welfare-to-work clients. My business partner, who had been an educator for over thirty years, was working with me to find creative ways to introduce their curriculum to the marketplace. We decided to attend an international conference on innovation to get some fresh ideas. One of the workshops we participated in was "effective Intelligence." The presenters, Jerry D. Rhodes and his colleague Ian Wigston, gave a dynamic presentation on this research-based cognitive process, which addressed the soft skills that I believed were essential to prepare our youth for life and work in the twenty-first century. Effective Intelligence proponents assert that thinking is a strategic skill that drives all other aspects of attitude, skill, and knowledge. They say that thinking is the most "transferable" competence with direct and indirect benefits to *every* activity. My partner and I were both so excited that we made a proposal to Jerry and Ian that we work together to adapt Effective Intelligence for K–12 education. Jerry and Ian were both based in the United Kingdom, so we agreed to meet them in Washington, DC, shortly thereafter to consider the possibilities.

About the same time, we hear about pending California legislation that would be more favorable to start-up charter schools. George Bernard Shaw, the British playwright and social reformer, is quoted as saying, "The people who get on in this world are the people who get up and look for the circumstances they want, and, if they can't find them, make them." We were fascinated and intrigued by the possibility of starting a school from scratch. We soon found ourselves in the United Kingdom, working with Jerry and Ian to become licensed and accredited to use Effective Intelligence to design and implement a charter school. Naturally, the vision for the school, its target population, the mission statement, and the educational program grew out of our experience—personally and professionally.

In writing the charter, the first thing we considered was the target population. My experiences with the *Up with People* high school gave me a true appreciation for Confucius's saying, "I hear and I forget. I see and I remember. I do and I understand." While most agree that all students benefit by doing, there are students for whom it is absolutely essential to their success. Odyssey is designed specifically to serve these students, whose learning styles are not well suited for a conventional classroom that is focused on paper-pencil activities, lectures, textbooks, and standardized tests. Students who are bored, unmotivated, and underachieving need a more engaging, "hands-on" learning environment that respects different ways of demonstrating their knowledge and abilities and isn't easily intimidated by their curiosity and creativity. An environment where, according the Plutarch, "The mind is not a vessel to be filled but a fire to be kindled."

One mission of Odyssey is to partner teachers, students, parents, and business and community volunteers to develop leaders and innovators for the knowledge-based global community in the twenty-first century. Another mission is to be responsive to the demands of the ever-changing, high-performance workplace. I was struck by an article in *Time* magazine in 1993, "The Tempting of America," in which Lance Morrow was quoted as saying, "America has entered the age of contingent or temporary worker, of the consultant and subcontractor, of the just-in-time workforce—fluid, flexible, disposable. This is the future. Its message is this: You are on your own. For good (sometimes) and ill (often) the workers of the future will constantly have to sell their skills, invent new relationships with employers who must, themselves, change and adapt constantly in order to survive in the ruthless global market." It is a stark reminder that the ability to cope with change and the ability to learn and unlearn may be the only job security on the horizon for our youth.

The design of Odyssey's education program was heavily influenced by the work of Jean Piaget (1896–1980). Piaget contends that "the principal goal of education in the schools should be creating men and women who are capable of doing new things, not simply repeating what other generations have done; men and women who are creative, inventive and discoverers, who can be critical and verify, and not accept everything they are offered." Odyssey is committed to facilitating the lifelong learning by skillful thinkers. The school's learning environment supports a *thinking-focused* program designed to develop timeless, transferable skills within three interdependent learning components: charter development, academic excellence, and future focus.

Keeping in mind our target population, we include in the learning environment a multiage setting designed to be student centered—focusing on what students need to succeed, engaging everyone as teachers and learners. Project-based learning opportunities provide a means for students to *take charge of their own learning* by actively planning, researching, and developing in-depth studies of topics of personal interest. Teachers and students evaluate learning on an ongoing basis through a variety of methods that honor different learning styles. A positive climate in the classroom is facilitated through peace education, conflict resolution, and peer mediation to build relationships and resolve conflicts. Parents are viewed as partners; Odyssey encourages and values parents' participation in their children's learning, at home and school.

By providing tools designed to improve the thinking performance of everyone in its learning community, Odyssey seeks to effect significant and fundamental change throughout the school, acknowledging that real change always requires a real paradigm shift in the way we think, the way we teach, and the way we learn. The most distinctive and compelling characteristic of the school design is the powerful combination of Effective Intelligence and the MicroSociety ® Program. Odyssey was awarded a $150,000 grant to assist in customizing Effective Intelligence for K–12 education. MicroSociety® is a national school reform model that transforms classrooms by providing a real-world context for academic learning. It also provides endless opportunities for developing critical-thinking skills. Students collaborate with parents, business volunteers, and teachers to create functioning small communities. Students have jobs that help them learn to run businesses, apply technology, develop government and social agencies, and create cultural and art organizations. Over time, students become immersed in the realities of free-market economy, including the detail of taxes, property concerns, income issues, and politics. MicroSociety® enables teachers to answer two persistent questions students ask: "Why do need to know this?" and "How do I fit in?"

THE CHARTER

As a change agent who consistently challenges assumptions about what's possible and consistently steps outside the box, I have been faced with numerous obstacles, land mines, and outright assaults throughout my life. My venture into the charter school arena has been no exception. The draft of Odyssey's charter was completed in August 1998, and we began the dialogue with the local school district with high hopes that the local school board would support and approve it. I had been involved in the recent reaccreditation process for the local high school over the previous year and thought I had gained some valuable insight into the unmet needs of students and the ways in which a charter school might address them. Over the next seven months, there seemed to be productive meetings with district staff to address their questions and concerns about the charter. We thought they were good faith negotiations. There were many refinements and revisions to the charter. During the review process, a critical decision was made to locate the school outside the district boundaries in response to concerns that were raised about the possibility that students from outside the district boundaries would be enrolled. However, we selected a site that was still close enough to effectively serve the students in the district who were interested in enrolling.

"Over the next seven months, there seemed to be productive meetings with district staff to address their questions and concerns about the charter. We thought they were good faith negotiations."

During this time, we also began our community outreach. I recently came across a quote from Ellen Frankfort that says, "Choice has always been a privilege of those who could afford to pay for it." This is especially true to the realm of education and is a particularly relevant issue as charter schools enter the market. Parents are conditioned when it comes to education. We had to introduce the community to the concept of school choice via "independent" public charter schools. We had to educate parents about what a charter school is and that a charter school is a *public, tuition-free* school *open to all* students. We learned that helping parents evaluate their choices, particularly those parents who historically have not had a choice, was more difficult than anticipated. All that being said, when the required charter petition was presented to the local school district, it contained far more signatures than the law required.

We held numerous mandatory parent orientation meetings to assist parents in determining whether Odyssey would be a good match for their children. We did not have a school to show parents, but we shared with them our vision and the distinctive characteristics of the school. My business partner engaged parents in an activity specifically designed to demonstrate the differences between a traditional classroom and what Odyssey intended to offer. At the conclusion of the orientation, parents were asked to carefully consider whether this would be a good fit for their children and whether they would be willing to be part of a start-up school, understanding there would be many expected and unexpected challenges. We later discovered that our efforts were subject to the limitation of words and difficulty associated with helping others fully grasp something new and unfamiliar.

We formally submitted our charter petition to the local school board in March 1999. While we certainly anticipated questions, we were not prepared for the intense resistance and, in some cases, hostility. Of particular concern was the perceived liability for special education students and the decision to locate the school outside the district boundaries. There was an unrelenting flurry of legal intervention on both sides; however, no amount of explanation, even by attorneys, could overcome their fears. The charter was denied.

Over 100 parents had come to the final hearing to voice their support for the school. Having the charter denied was incredibly frustrating and disappointing after all that had been invested and the strong community support that had been displayed. We had a second chance, however. California's new charter school legislation had a provision allowing a charter that had been denied by a local school district to be presented to a county board of education for approval.

Once again, the charter went through more scrutiny, this time by the county staff. There were more refinements and revisions, more legal interpretations and recommendations, and more refinements and revisions. Then, on May 25, 1999, the county board voted to approve Odyssey's charter. We were thrilled. Odyssey became the first school in the state to be granted a charter by a county board after being denied by a local school district. But there wasn't time to revel in our success; it was on to the next challenge.

THE OPENING STAGE

At a time when most education workers has already made commitments for the fall, Odyssey now had to secure a director of education, teachers, and support staff for a school that was anything but typical, where everyone would be a learner. Every employment ad ended with "Only Learners Need Apply." Interviews were designed to discern whether an individual was a good match for the school. Lacking a school to show them, we were again dependent on words, ours and those of the applicants. When the selection process was completed, we were confident we had found a dynamic team to birth the school. Yet not until "the rubber met the road" would we really be able to evaluate whether our choices were a good match for Odyssey. We would discover that not all were.

In July, the state formally issued Odyssey its status as a public charter school. During this time, the legislature and the California Department of Education were struggling with a new charter school funding model. It presented challenges for all charter schools in the state; however, yet again, Odyssey would become the test case for how the state would apply this new model to a school charter by a county board instead of a local school district. More tweaking of the legislation was required, and then everyone scrambled to figure out how to put it into action. Systemic change is never easy, especially when what is new doesn't fit into the existing system—by design. There were no easy or immediate answers. Even the uncertainty of the funding situation, we sought to obtain private funding to ensure that the school could open in early September, as scheduled. We had no history as an organization, so it was nothing short of miraculous that a financial institution granted the school an unsecured $250,000 line of credit, based solely on the anticipated public funds that, although delayed, were expected to show up by February. The private funds came just in time for the school to open as planned.

We had been fortunate to secure a five-year lease for facilities on a church campus across the street from the local community college. We had exclusive use of a two-story education building. Staff and parents labored for three weeks before the school opened to deal with significantly deferred maintenance issues and to make the building suitable for Odyssey's use. Everyone was relentless in his or her commitment to getting this done.

The "labor and delivery" process culminated when the school opened on September 7, 1999. Odyssey's 230 K–8 students, representing 167 families and coming from 12 different school districts within about a 15-mile radius, were diverse in every sense. Few knew one another before coming to Odyssey. About 100 other students were on a waiting list as a result of the school's lottery process. The staff of eighteen included ten teachers who had spent three weeks in August getting to know one another and preparing to open the school.

School furnishings were still arriving the first week of school. While teachers were busy creating a learning community within their classrooms, the administration and staff were dealing with the logistics of drop-off and pick-up of students in a safe and timely manner, class schedules, recess and lunch breaks, and how to make the best use of the limited playground and eating areas. Because the school had no cafeteria, parents were packing lunches every day.

By design my role had been more intensive during the design and development phase, my partner was to take a more active role once the school opened. However, somewhere between the charter being approved, the hiring of staff, our three-week training, and the school getting underway, my partner and I found ourselves strangely at odds on core issues. To everyone's surprise, as the reality of a nontraditional classroom and related school culture evolved, a clear difference quickly emerged in educational philosophy and administrative style, and in short order my partner resigned. I suddenly found myself in a position where I had to assume much more responsibility than anticipated. During this same time, our director of education had an unexpected health challenge and was out for six weeks. However, we had recently contracted with a consultant to assist us with our special education needs and she was able to step in during this time. It seemed as if I was working 24/7.

THE ODYSSEY ADVENTURE

In choosing the name "Odyssey" for the school, we may have set a course consistent with its definition, "long series of adventures filled with notable experience, hardships, etc." Over the next two years, like Christopher Columbus, we came to the realization that it may in fact be easier to discover a new world than to try to change the one that everyone knows so well. We gained firsthand knowledge that the difficulty is not so much in developing new ideas as in escaping from the old ones. Getting the OK to venture out where our independence and potential success might be perceived as a threat, competition, or divisive was just the beginning of our odyssey. There were many difficult decisions to be made about how to set appropriate expectations, for ourselves and others, and the ultimate challenge of adequately preparing for a journey that was moving us into more uncharted territory than we could have imagined with little lead-time and few start-up resources.

Over the years, I have come to realize that no amount of planning or experience can ever fully equip you for a new venture. Like Columbus, we left the familiarity of the shore on a new ship, with a new crew and 167 families on board (including 230 children)—all of whom had high hopes of a new world that would give them more freedom and opportunity (and fix all their problems in record time). We were learning to swim in the middle of the ocean, facing the natural perils of the sea and the indirect threats to our existence—efforts to undermine charter legislation, erode funding, and withhold or delay needed resources.

During our first year, best-laid plans immediately came face to face with the additional challenges associated with establishing a school culture from scratch, especially having opened with everything and everyone being new. This was especially true and understandable with the middle school students. They came to Odyssey with considerable baggage from their previous school experience, coupled with budding adolescence, further amplified by being in a new school that not only lacked a history and reputation to define its expectation but had an education program reflecting a different philosophy. A quote from Pogo says it well: "We are confronted with insurmountable opportunities." And we genuinely were approaching the challenges with that attitude, doing all we could to give change a chance. But change takes time and, more often than not, longer than some have the patience for. As a result, during the school year we were faced with turnover in some of our middle school staff and students.

"By the end of May, there was an attempted mutiny."

The first significant wave of discontent on our journey was in February 2000. In addition to our governing board, out initial governance structure included a fifteen-member advisory board: most were parents. This proved to be a major mistake. Although these parents were incredibly dedicated and gave way above and beyond expectations, what began as valuable help soon grew into a sense of entitlement. A number of parents began to encroach into areas that were not appropriate for parental involvement, and soon they were attempting to micromanage the school. This small, yet, powerful contingent of parents (who were primarily Anglo and from a private school setting) made demands to get the "undesirables" (those who didn't look or act like them and, ironically, those who needed Odyssey the most) to conform to their expectations within three weeks, or they would be thrown overboard, so to speak. With support of the governing board and staff, I followed our map (our charter), compass (the needs of our targeted students), and stars (our ultimate vision). Over the next three months, this stand resulted in waves of unrelenting attacks that at times became very personal and vicious.

By the end of May, there was an attempted mutiny initiated by seven families who enlisted the aid of those who had the power to end our journey (county staff, county board members, and local elected officials). We quickly scrambled to find our life preservers, naively thinking they were in the hundred or so families who signed a petition supporting the school, and in our thorough response to the complaints. But alas, it would take an exhausting six months of intense work, an unwavering resolve, amendments to our charter, and significant and costly legal intervention to preserve our school without compromising its vision.

During our first year, another significant wave came in the form of special education. While our director of education had twenty-five years of experience in meeting the needs of students with special needs, for practical reasons we had made a decision to outsource our special education service for at least the first year. Our commitment to our special education students was high; however, we were faced with unacceptable turnover in service providers, now beyond our control. As a result, our relationship with the contractor was strained at best. This took its toll on service delivery.

We also experienced difficulties educating parents on the full inclusion model to which we were so committed. In addition, parent expectations were probably unrealistic for a first-year, start-up school. They were further complicated by the fact that most came to Odyssey with a long history of needs not being met by their home district. Of course, Odyssey was expected to fix these problems without delay. We were also faced with a higher than normal percentage of students with a wide array of special education needs. Worse yet, we did not receive any special education funding until spring. Fortunately, we were able to absorb these costs with our loan. No doubt, all of these challenges contributed to two parents filing for due process, unfortunately in a hostile manner. Even more problematic, driven by potential or perceived liability, we suddenly found everyone in the system taking sides rather than working together to resolve all the related issues. Once again, Odyssey was forced to seek what turned out to be costly legal intervention, but we were able to settle the cases responsibly.

"The challenge of finding a good match, whether in our staffing or in our students, is by far the most important struggle we have."

In the end, we certainly echoed Friedrich Nietzsche's words: "that which does not kill us makes us stronger." We went into our second year stronger and wiser. The challenge of finding a good match, whether in our staffing or in our students, is by far the most important struggle we have, in light of the innovative nature of our charter. We learned the hard way that parents always filter the information presented at our two-hour, mandatory orientations through their own understanding, previous experiences, hopes, and desires, and in some cases with their own agendas. As we prepared for our second year, we regrouped and worked harder, and I believe smarter, to recruit teachers and students who were up for the new challenges before us on the next leg of our journey. As a result of the sifting-out process at the end of our first year, we began the new term with about seventy new families and four new teachers. Not surprisingly, it made a significant difference in the look and feel of our campus and our classrooms. We also made a decision to hire a full inclusion specialist and to contract our only special service (e.g., speech and language). This provided the stability our students needed and ensured that our special education services were in concert with the distinctive characteristics of our charter.

By January, we had reconfigured our governance structure, which resulted in one governing body. The governing board is a policy-level board and is truly a representative body. Stakeholders include three community members, the founder/executive director, one teacher, and two parents (one K–4 representative and one 5–8 representative). This has proven to be a tremendous improvement and provides the support needed by the administration without encroaching on the day-to-day operations of the school.

By the spring, parents had finally recuperated from the previous challenges and were ready to put together a parent organization. They formed the Odyssey Parent Participation Group and established working committees to support various activities within the school, and they play an important role in the success of our school.

"There were remarkable turnarounds with students whom many would have gladly thrown overboard. It made everything we went through worthwhile."

Throughout our second year, we learned to enjoy our journey. We built the foundation for a strong community by taking important steps toward embracing our differences and resolving our conflicts in a productive and respectful manner. Periodically those who had abandoned ship at the end of our first year continued to criticize and attempt to undermine our efforts. Fortunately, it was ineffective in the light of the critical mass of supportive parents, a team of professionals, who were united in their mission, and county staff who seemed to recognize our commitment of continuous improvement.

During our first two years in operation, in the midst of and despite the challenges, students were finding success and taking responsibility for their learning. There were remarkable turnarounds with students whom many would have gladly thrown overboard. It made everything we went through worthwhile.

The governing board graciously granted me a study leave at the end of the school year. The winds appeared calm; there seemed to be a fair sea before us—was that land on the horizon? As I reflected on our first two years, I felt blessed that we had come so far. We had a strong team, including our governing board, staff, parents, and students who were well equipped for the next leg of the journey. I invited our director of education, who was not only a valued colleague but had quickly become a good friend to join me toward the end of the week to strategize preparations for the fall. That is when I learned that she had been offered an opportunity to be a part of a new special education school and hoped I would support her in that move. After I caught my breath, I realized the she and Odyssey were in a different stage of development, and perhaps our needs were now different.

It was almost July. How were we to find just the right educational leadership? As has happened so often in my life, and the life of our school, providence set in. An individual immediately came to mind, but would she even consider a change, let alone on such short notice? As I began to reach out to others who might know of individuals who might be good candidates, her resume appeared on the top of the stack. Within weeks she was on board. As an experienced educator who has been a leader in the field of progressive education, she brings the depth of knowledge and experience we need to enter the new world with the tools and resources needed to fulfill our vision.

We also had a change in our administrative support at the end of our second year. Our new office manager/registrar was learning the ins and outs of school operations. As the founder and executive director of the school, I had maintained my 24/7 role for over two years without a significant break. While I realized it wasn't healthy, I found it difficult to break the cycle. I was looking forward to entering the new school year with a strong leadership team that would help me shift into a new role. I was hopeful that these two new individuals would be capable of carrying the day-to-day operations and leadership at the school. The governing board was affirming that I needed to move back into the development mode. I envisioned becoming the ultimate "resource choreographer."

What happened next not only forced the issue but was life changing and may have even been lifesaving for me. On the last day of July, we held a parent orientation meeting in the evening. It was late and I was tired. I was carrying things down the stairs to my office when I lost my footing, hit the concrete ground full force, and shattered by right heel. I spent the first six weeks in bed, three months in a wheelchair and crutches, and will be on crutches for several more months. While I would never wish this on anyone, it has shown me so much. I have certainly gained a whole new perspective on mobility issues. And I have finally been able to let go of the 24/7 role. My laptop, e-mail, and phone allow me to work from home, giving me time to regroup and prepare for my shifting role.

My new colleagues rose to the occasion in every way. They provide exceptional leadership and allow me to support and mentor them in their new roles. The real blessing for me personally and professionally has been to see the growth and maturing of the governing board parents, staff, and students as they take ownership of the vision and make it more and more a reality every day. As I am becoming more mobile, I will be moving out in the community and am excited that my dream of becoming the "resource choreographer" will soon be realized.

In our third year, I believe we have finally made landfall. What challenges do we face as we embrace the new world? We have no doubt made many mistakes in our first two years, and we will make new ones as we seek to make this new world our own. Mahatma Gandhi was adamant in stating: "Freedom is not worth having if it does not include the freedom to make mistakes." California's charter school legislation offers Odyssey and others the freedom to innovate in exchange for great accountability, and yet, with innovation, mistakes are a guaranteed part of the process. They are absolutely necessary if real and lasting change is to take place. We often find ourselves in a precarious position—under a high-powered microscope that zooms in on any and all mistakes, in a system that is historically "risk adverse." All too often, the systems' reaction to something new and unfamiliar, especially when mistakes are being made, is to legislate it back into something that fits the standard paradigm. Learning how to survive in these waters and finding creative and constructive ways to work together for the benefit of the children will be essential to our very existence as we move forward.

Chapter 4

Staying the Course as the Odyssey Continues

Kathleen O'Sullivan started Odyssey Charter School nearly twenty years ago. While in its infancy, she had commented, "The real blessing for me personally and professionally has been to see the growth and maturing of the governing board, parents, staff, and students as they take ownership of the vision and make it more and more a reality every day." Growth of the school and those within it did, in fact, occur and Kathleen was able to step back and hand the journey over to other educational leaders as Odyssey continued its voyage.

Odyssey Charter School has more than doubled in size. It has grown from an opening student population of 230 K–8 students on September 7, 1999, representing 167 families located in a leased church building, to its current 6-acre campus serving almost 500 students. The size of the faculty and staff has grown from a mere eighteen devoted explorers in 1999, to fifty-seven committed professionals who met the criterion of "Only Learners Need Apply."

"The real blessing for me personally and professionally has been to see the growth and maturing of the governing board, parents, staff, and students as they take ownership of the vision and make it more and more a reality every day."

Lauren O'Neill is now the Executive Director of Odyssey, a role she has held since 2007. O'Neill, was one was of the founding eighteen faculty members in 1999. Since then, she has held many different roles at Odyssey leading up to Executive Director. According to the charter school's website, as Odyssey's Executive Director over the past decade, she has overseen much school growth, ensured students' learning and sustained achievement, all the while using the initial school mission as the compass.

Today the mission and vision of Odyssey has evolved and expanded a bit beyond the founders' original charter, but it is still the rudder of their ship. The original charter document called for "providing all students with the opportunity to guide their own learning in a student-centered, project-based learning environment in a positive climate built on positive relationships." The goal was to give students the skills needed in the twenty-first century through learning opportunities at school and at home.

Today's charter mission reads, "Our mission is to develop students who are active in their learning, aware of their interests, and who seek to expand and explore their knowledge through dynamic collaboration with peers and teachers within an academic setting and the larger community." This is achieved in primarily multi-age classrooms by creating an active and engaging learning environment based on a workshop format. Odyssey envisions the workshop model as an opportunity for student choice within an environment of academic excellence.

The mission reflects a somewhat stronger focus on students taking responsibility for their learning through engaging with faculty and fellow students in school and throughout their community, however the specific words "project-based learning" have been omitted. The school does remain focused on each individual student and meeting their needs for growth through hands-on, project-based learning opportunities. The school has also maintained its commitment to a diverse student population; today's students represent 45 percent white, 30 percent Hispanic, 10 percent Black, and another 15 percent mixed.

While the mission and vision today are similar to that of 1999, the school itself has changed notably through three successful charter renewals, largely due to growth. Along with the hiring of new faculty to accommodate increased numbers of students, co-curricular programs in Art, Gardening, Physical Education, and technology have been developed. These additional options better serve their diverse student population but are still relatively project-based in nature. Campus technology and infrastructure have been upgraded, and facilities continue to be improved with additions such as playgrounds and the refurbishing of campus bungalows.

The board and school leadership is also gearing up for the addition of a second campus next year. Lauren O'Neill has been a part of the Odyssey's evolution from the first opening classrooms to the present overall growing organization.

"Clearly a charter school advocate, she added that one way charter school leadership has changed over time is that there are additional demands on charter leaders; some of them are political."

FOCUS ON LEADERSHIP

In a 2016 interview Lauren gave us some insights into her journey at Odyssey over the past two decades and shared some of her thoughts about the future. When asked how she views her current work in education, Lauren replied that she harbors "a passion for quality public education choice and the possibility for reform through the charter school movement." Clearly a charter school advocate, she added that one way charter school leadership has changed over time is that there are additional demands on charter leaders; some of them are political. "The need and responsibility to establish, maintain, and support political leaders and legislation that supports the charter school movement as a whole is necessary. This can often take time away from focusing on student learning and can be burdensome on small independent schools. Thus, it is paramount to have a strong working relationship with your charter authorizer."

In this way, the role resembles more that of a district superintendent than a school principal. In retrospect, the Odyssey leadership reflected that taking more of an ABS (Arts-Based School) approach from the onset might have made their road less bumpy, but they now enjoy an equally collegial relationship with their district rather than the difficult relationship of the early years.

The present state of charter leadership in California requires double reporting and compliance to authorizers as well as state and federal agencies; accountability has intensified. As a consequence, when asked if the idea of founding a charter school is becoming more or less attractive than it was two decades ago, O'Neill answered, "I certainly think it is becoming more and more difficult to establish a single operator charter school and overall more difficult to receive approval on a petition." However, Prop 39 has made it somewhat easier to obtain facilities.

Most of Lauren's preparation for her leadership position occurred over time on the job. She had been a founding teacher at Odyssey, served on the board, and took on leadership roles in addition to her classroom responsibilities along the way. She worked with the team of faculty and new administration in the rewriting of the charter for its first renewal process. "All of these experiences contributed to my preparation when I transitioned into the Executive Director position after 7 years"; however, she stated that "the transition was difficult and overwhelming. Fortunately, the previous Executive Director [Kathleen O'Sullivan] remained as a consultant during the first transitional year for support and this was tremendously beneficial."

"Empowering teachers is key to building successful school communities, and I believe Odyssey's success can be attributed to including the teacher voice in decisions."

As far as her own leadership style or philosophy, her top criteria was "it is important to involve all stakeholders in the decision making process. Empowering teachers is key to building successful school communities, and I believe Odyssey's success can be attributed to including the teacher voice in decisions." Clearly this priority was shared as she progressed from a role of teacher giving input to a director receiving input from her teachers.

When asked what preparation programs for charter leaders should focus on, she mentioned that she was not aware of any preparation programs specifically for charter leaders. However, she suggested that ideally "leadership experience and experience as a classroom teacher should be required for charter leaders. I think good preparation programs include internships at school sites so aspiring charter leaders can work with a mentor prior to assuming leading their own school environment." She added that experience with governance and managing boards is paramount for the success of charter school leadership.

And Odyssey is still thriving. Their transition to the Common Core curriculum was relatively smooth as demonstrated in their student test scores on the California Assessment of Student Performance and Progress state exams (CAASPP). Seventy-eight percent of students met and exceeded standards in English Language Arts, and sixty-five percent of students met and exceeded math standards.

Over the past five years the waitlist for the school has exceeded 500 students for approximately only fifty openings. Their retention rate is approximately 98 percent which has caused their admission rate to be roughly less than 10 percent. Therefore, they are currently in the process of opening a second school of about 450 students to continue to provide a high-quality public school of choice in a nearby community. Their petition received approval to open a second school, beginning with grades TK–3 in the fall of 2018.

"And Odyssey is still thriving."

With over two decades of successful experience now, they believe they have the capacity, student/family interest, practical knowledge, and perhaps most importantly, the passion for quality to continue to be successful. Clearly their community agrees.

Chapter 5

Darkness Before Dawn

The Arts-Based Elementary School

HAL JOHNSON, BB&T

Hal Johnson became involved with the Sawtooth Center for Visual Art in 1994. The Arts-Based Elementary School (ABES) concept grew out of the strategic planning process conducted with the Sawtooth Center board. The Sawtooth Center served as an incubator for the school until it became a separate organization in 1999. Since 2001, Johnson has been an executive vice president of BB&T, one of the nation's twelve largest bank holding companies. His tenure with the company began in 1985 when Southern National Corporation hired him as a marketing research assistant. Two years later, he was promoted to the position of marketing director for the corporation. His creativity in this role produced the slogan "You can tell we want your business." This tag line embodied the spirit of SNC's corporate values and continues to be used in current marketing promotions. In 1989, he developed a strategic planning department. Working with the bank's executive management and the corporation's board of directors, he helped shape the future of Southern National through his work with the corporation's strategic plans and acquisition strategy. He has been involved in 98 acquisitions, including 29 banks and thrifts, 52 insurance agencies, and 17 nonbank companies. He has seen the company grow in asset size from $20 billion to over $90 billion.

The Arts-Based Elementary School (ABES) is located in Winston-Salem, North Carolina, a city of about 285,000 in a region (the Piedmont Triad Region of North Carolina) of about 1.2 million. Winston-Salem has a national reputation as being a community steeped in the arts. That reputation is built on a heritage of strong funding for the arts by RJ Reynolds, Hanes, and Wachovia. In fact, Winston-Salem bills itself as the "City of the Arts."

41

THE SEED

ABES began as a seed concept in 1996. At the time, I was a board member and the strategic planning chair for the Sawtooth Center for Visual Art in Winston-Salem. The Sawtooth Center is a Visual Art School that provides training for a range of interests from the hobbyist to the professional. The school's mission is to train artists, not to provide a formal education or grant degrees.

We were conducting a strategy session for the organization, trying to set the course for the organization's next five years in the face of declining funding for the arts, increasing demands for our services, and the desire to expand our reach in the community. The planning session was facilitated by Arthur Andersen and had representatives from the board and staff of the Sawtooth organization, the Winston-Salem Arts Council (a major source of funds for the organization), and the community at large. The session suggested many themes for the Sawtooth Center to develop, one of which was the idea of becoming a degree-granting institution.

"Jim and I became energized about combining ... arts-based reforms in education with the idea of expanding ... to become a degree-granting organization."

During the period when the brainstorming session was held, legislation permitting charter schools in North Carolina was at the conceptual stage. Much discussion followed about expanding Sawtooth's scope to become a degree-granting institution. As a board, we also explored many of the other options developed during the session for expanding the reach of Sawtooth.

During the time we were working on implementing programs that were developed at the planning session, Jim Sanders, the executive director of the Sawtooth Center, started to pursue a doctorate in educational curriculum and instruction. Jim and I became energized about combining the research he was undertaking in arts-based reforms in education with the idea of expanding Sawtooth's reach to become a degree-granting organization.

"Early on in the process of forming the school, we made philosophical decisions that would prove critical in the years to come."

We followed the progress of charter legislation in the North Carolina General Assembly and educated the Sawtooth board on what was happening with the charter school movement. We encouraged the board to consider setting up a sister organization to run the school. The Sawtooth board reviewed the North Carolina charter school legislation when it was enacted, and additional debate on Sawtooth becoming the sponsor for a charter school ensued. We considered structures in which a common holding company would be created and the Sawtooth Center for Visual Art and the Arts-Based Elementary School would be sister organizations under its common umbrella. Ultimately the Sawtooth board agreed to allow Jim to use some of his time as an employee of Sawtooth to write the charter and submit it for approval. However, the Sawtooth board did not want to be the sponsoring organization for ABES.

EARLY ORGANIZATION

Jim and I formed an organizing committee and began work. Early on in the process of forming the school, we made philosophical decisions that would prove critical in the years to come. Just how critical these choices would be we could not have ever conceived at this early stage.

We spelled out the basic philosophy for the school. Jim was the primary architect of the vision as we began to develop our concepts:

- The school would serve K–5 and the curriculum would be delivered using the arts (music, dance, visual art, theater).
- The school would strive for a racial balance that reflected the larger community (67 percent white, 26 percent African American, 7 percent Hispanic).
- The school would be located in a racially neutral site in downtown Winston-Salem within easy reach of the city's arts organizations.
- The school's campus would extend to include the entire city.
- Students would learn how to navigate an urban landscape.
- Each child would develop and build upon an educational portfolio as they progressed through their educational experience from kindergarten through fifth grade.
- The school would become a partner with the city's arts organizations and would also seek out other partnerships that could strengthen its curriculum.

SECURING THE CHARTER

There are two ways to submit a charter application in North Carolina. One can submit it either to the local education authority (LEA), that is, the local public school board, or one can submit it directly to the North Carolina Department of Public Instruction. Most charter schools bypass the LEA in favor of applying directly to the state. There are three reasons for this pattern: (1) if the LEA turns down your charter application, you cannot appeal to the state; (2) most charter schools maintain adversarial relationships with their LEA; and (3) if you submit through your LEA and they approve it, the application still needs to be approved by the state, thus adding another level of approval.

The ABES board did not believe it served our interests to be at odds with our LEA, and thus we submitted our charter application to the Winston-Salem Forsyth County School Board: This decision was also consistent with our mission of seeking local partnerships that could strengthen our school. The LEA unanimously endorsed our charter application and sent it on to the state for consideration. The local Chamber of Commerce also endorsed our application to the LEA and to the state. One of the lessons we would come to learn is that you can never have too many friends and allies.

Our charter was granted in early 2000 and we had permission to open our school in the *fall* of 2000. Our plans, however, called for a year of ground work, with the school scheduled to open for the 2001–02 school year. Our next challenge was to find a suitable building for the school.

"One of the lessons we would come to learn is that you can never have too many friends and allies."

FINDING PHILANTHROPY DIFFICULT

My leadership role with ABES was about to begin in earnest. Jim asked if I would serve as chairman of the board of the new organization that was to be formed to take the concept of an arts-based charter school forward. We started with all the usual perfunctory tasks, forming a corporation, writing bylaws, recruiting board members, and so forth.

We put together a task list of all the critical functions to be accomplished in order to open the school. We recruited a *very* strong board that provided the organization with expertise in many different disciplines, as well as a team of people who were willing to roll up their sleeves and work hard together. Our initial board consisted of individuals such as Peter Perret, the conductor of the Winston-Salem symphony and creator of the Bolton Project, a proven arts-based reform based on the positive impact of music on developing the brain. Other founding members came from such organizations as Wake Forest University, Volvo Trucks, BB&T Corporation (a major bank), the United Way of Forsyth County, the Wake Forest University School of Medicine, Womble Carlyle Sandridge & Rice (a major law firm), American Express, the Winston-Salem Housing Authority, and the community at large. Thus, we had a strong cross section of academics, business professionals, and supportive community volunteers.

We began to work on many things concurrently, meeting as a board every two weeks and feeling as if we were all holding a second job. We began to hold student recruitment meetings at the downtown public library during the winter of 2000–01. We had a good response from parents interested in putting their children in the school when it opened. We also embarked on what would turn out to be our most difficult task, finding a building to house the school.

"We learned that our city building code for a downtown school was much more restrictive than state requirements.... Collectively, these standards removed almost every site from consideration."

In keeping with our founding principles, we wanted to secure a building in downtown Winston-Salem within easy reach of the arts venues and on ground that would be considered racially and socioeconomically neutral. We recruited a real estate professional to our board (the head of facilities for a major corporation) and retained a local commercial real estate broker to review space options.

As we toured available buildings, it became apparent that the task of finding space that was both suitable and desirable was not going to be easy. We learned that our city building code for a downtown school was much more restrictive than state requirements. The code requires 100 square feet per child, a 5,000 square foot playground on site, and the kindergarten and first-grade classrooms on ground level, with two exits per classroom. Collectively, these standards removed almost every site from consideration.

We began to focus in on the Lewey building, in the heart of the central business district, which seemed to satisfy all the required code issues. We hired an architect to lay out the floor space and determined the building would work. We then began to negotiate a lease with the building owners. During the negotiations, which were proceeding as planned, we had the architect complete construction drawings and put the project out to bid with three contractors. The bids came in at about the cost expected, and we selected a contractor to do the work.

"We had 120 families ready to send their children to the school. Delivering the news that we would not be able to open in the fall was one of the hardest things we had to do."

We finalized the negotiations on the building lease, including an upfit allowance sufficient to do the majority of the renovation work that would be needed. Our attorney worked through the final details, and the lease was ready to be signed when, at the last minute, the building owners (an out-of-state group) pulled out of the transaction. It was now late spring of 2001. At this point, it was going to be almost impossible to find a new location and get it ready to open a school in by fall. The board worked feverishly to try to identify another building. We found one possible location but decided that the building's current use and its designation as a historic landmark would preclude making the necessary changes within the time remaining to get the project done.

"Many alliances were formed during this ongoing trial by fire that would play a major role in the ultimate success of the school."

We had 120 families ready to send their children to the school. Delivering the news that we would not be able to open in the fall was one of the hardest things we had to do. However, we felt that we had an obligation to the families to let them know in enough time that they were not shut out of all their other education alternatives. We continued to maintain a dialogue with our families by e-mail and with face-to-face meetings over the course of the next year as we started over on the building search. It would have been easy to throw in the towel and blame our failure on an unfortunate real estate transaction, but to quote NASA: "Failure was not an option."

THE SEARCH CONTINUES

Many alliances were formed during this ongoing trial by fire that would play a major role in the ultimate success of the school. The two individuals who were responsible for creating our unique curriculum were the heads of two major art organizations in Winston-Salem. Jim Sanders was the executive director of the Sawtooth Center for Visual Art and Peter Perret was the conductor for the Winston-Salem Symphony. Both of these individuals had long records of providing services to the public school system in the county through their respective organizations.

In the spring of 2002, the Winston-Salem Forsyth County School (WSFCS) system was awarded a federal grant to create an arts-based magnet school in the district. A staff member responsible for the magnet program at the WSFCS system contacted Peter Perret to determine if the ABES board would be interested in supplying the curriculum for the magnet school. This eventually led to meetings with the senior staff at the WSFCS system, including the superintendent, Dr. Don Martin. A proposal was developed that called for the magnet school to become a district-run charter school to be managed by the ABES board, which would have a dotted-line relationship with the WSFCS board instead of being entirely independent, as with most charter schools. The ABES board had to decide if it should join forces with the WSFCS system to run one of its schools under this arrangement.

"We had to decide between making a major financial commitment ... or accepting somewhat less autonomy in a relationship with a strong partner who would be a major asset to ... our program."

We had identified a building (a facility we called the sewing building) that would be an excellent home for our school, and the board was divided between developing our own building or joining forces with the WSFCS system. We had to decide between making a major financial commitment in the face of an unsuccessful attempt at opening the previous year or accepting somewhat less autonomy in a relationship with a strong partner who would be a major asset to building our program.

We knew that the task of converting the designated public school location to a charter school would not be easy. The school was in an impoverished part of town and adjacent to a large public housing neighborhood and a major highway. We held meetings at the school to determine the interest of our constituents as well as the residents of the neighborhoods surrounding the school that would be impacted by the change from a community "zone" school to districtwide magnet.

Our board voted to pursue this opportunity with WSFCS. We decided that our program could reach more children and that we would be removed from the administrative burdens of running a school under this arrangement. We were also confident in the strength of our curriculum and decided that if it proved itself in this setting, it would become an indisputable model to apply to a broader universe of schools and students.

Little did we know, we were blazing new trails that were not anticipated under the current charter law. To do what we wanted to do would require an affirmative vote of the majority of the current families at the school that was to become a district-run charter, a similar majority vote by the school's teachers, and a change in the state's charter law to allow the district to establish another LEA under its umbrella. The board, in collaboration with the staff of the WSFCS system, now found itself lobbying in Raleigh, the state capital, for a change to the law and politicking with the community being served by the school to support a change of the school to a district-run charter.

The boards of both the ABES organization and the WSFCS system worked hard to make this proposal work. The delegation of elected officials from our county was supportive of trying to change the legislation to allow our proposal to work. We met with the staff of the state's Department of Public Instruction and Division of Charter Schools to work out the details of what would be required to make this proposal work. As with most things dealing with politics and bureaucratic organizations, there were those who did not support a change to the status quo, but we generally found people to be very supportive of our concept to blaze new ground.

The people involved with administering the state's charter program were most supportive and very excited about seeing the possibility of collaboration between the traditional public school sector and the charter school movement. We knew if we were successful with our vote at the public school, the Forsyth County delegation was willing to sponsor what is known as a local bill (a change in the law that only applies to one particular situation in a single community) in the state house to allow our partnership with WSFCS to move forward until such time as we could garner enough legislative support to change the state charter law applicable to all charter schools.

"Unfortunately we were viewed as outsiders trying to 'take away a community asset' rather than benefactors trying to bring a unique and positive program to the community school."

On the local scene, we held many meetings at the school to try to win the hearts of the local community. Unfortunately, we were viewed as outsiders trying to "take away a community asset" rather than benefactors trying to bring a unique and positive program to the community school. Our campaign to win the hearts of the community included door-to-door canvassing, meeting with local leaders from the housing project neighborhood, and open meetings at the school. This entire process became a local media story with much unflattering coverage. When the voting was done, the staff of the public school voted in favor of the conversion, but we lost the school-family vote by the slimmest of margins; the vote was almost evenly split. It was now late spring of 2002.

IT'S ALWAYS DARKEST BEFORE THE DAWN

During the time our board spent trying to make the district-run charter work, I formed a cooperative working relationship with Dr. Don Martin, WSFCS superintendent. Don not only cares about the children and the quality of education but is willing to try new things to advance the education options in the county. He deserves a full measure of credit for the ultimate survival of our program, because without his far-reaching support and that of his staff, we would have been defeated at this point.

Excited about the ABES program, Don continued to meet with Jim, Peter, and me to look for a solution that would allow us to implement our program. After much exploration, Don offered to lease us six classrooms in an under-utilized public school. Additionally, he offered to provide the administrative support of his organization to allow us to focus on picking up the pieces of our badly battered organization and try to recruit enough students, buy furniture, and so on, to salvage our next school year that was to begin in a few short months. Our board decided to take this opportunity to bring our program to life.

"Without [the superintendent's] far-reaching support and that of his staff, we would have been defeated at this point."

Our board went to Atkins Middle School, where we would be leasing the six classrooms. These rooms represented an entire hallway on the ground floor of the three-story middle school. At a meeting held with the facility and administrative staff of the school, many questions were asked about our school and our intentions. There was much concern about what our program might mean for them in the long term. The administration at the school was not sure what to make of this arrangement, which they viewed as "the heavy hand of the central office" imposing its will on their school.

As was our modus operandi by now, we set out to develop a good working relationship with our new hosts. We invited a person of their choosing to join our board of directors. They nominated the assistant principal to our board. This connection turned out to be a valuable resource for us, as she counseled us on many issues related to the school we were in, education law, and the internal workings of our new partner, the WSFCS system, as we set about the job of trying to get our school open. I worked to build a personal relationship with the principal of the school in order to try to create an avenue to promote positive cross pollination and effective conflict resolution, since both would likely be needed during the year.

We obtained donated furniture from many businesses around town and purchased surplus furniture from the WSFCS system. We had to use one classroom for office space, so we decided to open with five classes: one kindergarten, two first grades, one second grade, and one third grade. With our curriculum design providing a target of fifteen and a maximum of eighteen children per class, we knew the year would be difficult financially, as it would be hard to pay for our administrative staff and other overhead costs with a target enrollment of seventy-five. We opened the school with sixty-eight children, about half of whom were from the original group of parents that had wanted to join our school from the beginning. Jim Sanders served as a part-time principal while continuing to serve as the executive director of the

Sawtooth Center. We hired our teaching staff, one full-time administrator, and an administrative assistant. Our total staff consisted of seven full-time employees and Jim as our part-time principal.

"The bathrooms were located on a different hall in a section of the school used by middle school students. We programmed 'bathroom breaks' into our daily routine, lining up the children and trying to make a fun adventure out of our hike down the hall."

Our first year was marked by the normal bumps you would expect with any new business. Through it all, the board and staff focused on creating a successful year for the students. Funding worries plagued our school in the early part of the year; we did not want to spend money we did not have, and thus our program was lean through the first half of the year. The board worked diligently on fund raising, but it was difficult; the community did not yet see our program as stable enough to be worthy of financial support. But the board was committed to making the program a success and worked tirelessly and resourcefully to overcome the challenges and make sure the classroom experience for the children was first rate.

Our "school within a school" at Atkins created additional challenges and opportunities for us during the year. The wing of the school where our classrooms were located was a significant distance from the nearest bathrooms. The bathrooms were located on a different hall in a section of the school used by middle school students. We programmed "bathroom breaks" into our daily routine, lining up the children and trying to make a fun adventure out of our hike down the hall. This procedure had to be coordinated so it would not take place while the middle school students were making a classroom change.

The building had many wonderful attributes that a program like ours could never have afforded. Sterling Garris, the principal of our host school, let us make use of their piano lab, gave us almost exclusive rights to a second gymnasium in the building, and allowed us to put on productions in the school's beautifully renovated auditorium. The staff of the school was *very* accommodating and gracious, going above and beyond the call of duty to help us.

In making the space available for us, the principal of the school had to relocate all his sixth-grade teachers. In an attempt to let them know we understood and appreciated the sacrifice they made for us, at Thanksgiving we made a gift of a turkey to each sixth-grade teacher and each administrator in the school. This gesture of appreciation and recognition was *very* warmly received.

THINGS BEGIN TO TURN, BUT
CHALLENGES CONTINUE

In early winter 2002, the Office of Charter Schools informed us that we were eligible for a portion of a federal start-up grant that they had applied for and received. We completed an application to the state charter office and were awarded $177,000 in additional funds. It was a major lift to our program. We immediately hired assistants for the classrooms and a curriculum coordinator (Robin Hollis, who would eventually be named full-time principal) to work with our dedicated but nearly burned out crew of teachers. Without constant money worries, things definitely took a turn for the better, and our program began to get legs. Through the remainder of the year, we received four other grants.

"The building owners began to get excited about our school. . . . [They] became our greatest financial benefactors. We worked out a lease arrangement that was very favorable to our school."

During the year, we recruited another facilities expert to our board, Mary Benton, an executive with Novant Health, a large hospital corporation headquartered in our community. It turned out that one of the most promising buildings we had reviewed during our facilities search, the sewing building, was owned by two gentlemen with whom Mary had done a lot of work. Mary opened negotiations with the building owners about moving the school to their building.

The building owners began to get excited about our school, but it was difficult to get them excited about our financial position. We had a very strong board with many community leaders, but a shaky history. The relocation of the school from our five-classroom "school within a school" to their building would be but one more change dynamic in the life of our fledgling organization. Based on the strength of our board, Mary's relationship with the owners, and their excitement for our program, they decided to support our cause and became our greatest financial benefactors. We worked out a lease arrangement that was very favorable to our school, based on a per enrolled student cost (with a minimum lease cost based on 150 children), and a generous unfit allowance.

"The grant was significant not only for its financial support but as a signal that the community now saw our organization as having proved itself worthy of support."

In February 2003, we had a media event to announce our new location and began to recruit our expanded student body for the 2003–2004 school year.

We decided not to build out the entire space the first year to help limit our (and the building owners') financial exposure. We decided to expand to ten classrooms, with a maximum enrollment of 180 students. By mid-June 2003, we had reached 180 enrolled students and had a waiting list for every class.

Toward the end of the school year, ABES was notified that we had been granted funds from the Hanes Foundation. The grant was significant not only for its financial support but as a signal that the community now saw our organization as having proved itself worthy of support.

OTHER FIRST-YEAR PROBLEMS AND BLESSINGS

In the last quarter of the school year, our enrollment fell to sixty-two students. Under the state's charter legislation, a school must maintain sixty-five or more children or be put on probation. Well, you guessed it; we received a letter from the Office of Charter Schools informing us we were out of compliance.

This followed a string of personnel-related issues that we had to deal with in our first year. We had to deal with a staff member who left because she was not a good fit for our school. She filed a complaint with the state, saying that we did not provide services called for by her child's individualized education plan (IEP) in a timely fashion. We successfully navigated these problems but learned much about the myriad of education laws and regulations during the year. We also learned what we wanted the staff and leadership of our school to resemble the following year.

We were blessed to find an exceptional principal that first year. Robin Hollis, our curriculum coordinator, was named principal in early spring of 2003. She had fallen in love with our school and was a perfect person for the job. Through her work with the school during the second half of our inaugural year, she prepared us well for our second (upcoming) year. She is largely responsible for the expansion of our student body; she inspired confidence in prospective parents as they toured our school during the student recruitment process for our second year. We also learned our teacher selection process in the first year was not optimal. We created an abstract from the examples of our most successful classroom teachers and used that to create a teacher profile as we hired our staff for year two.

Our building continued to be a challenge as we progressed through the upfit. Our plans fell under the newly enacted International Building Code. Code requirements imposed on the renovation by the new international code and our city building department caused the project to run over budget by $75,000. We also ran into problems with the adjacent land owner. The building we were renovating was an all-brick shell. We planned on adding windows as part of the renovation. Because the building sits on the property line, our workers needed to set up their scaffold on the adjacent property to add windows on one side of the building. Despite a campaign of neighborly courtesies by ABES, the neighboring land owner refused the contractor access to his property. Thus, it seems nothing comes easy.

LESSONS LEARNED

Our first year of operations was full of lessons, both positive and negative. As a board and an organization, we have learned the power of persistence and the value of the collective strength that comes from a board composed of dedicated and competent people from a multitude of disciplines. We have learned that parents have innumerable talents and are eager to support their kids' school. We also learned that a process often builds upon its history and that you have to make good decisions that are consistent with your mission from the beginning.

As we talked with our parents at the end of our first year, it became evident that the strength of our curriculum design was sound. Moreover, parents told us that the challenges the school and the board faced were not felt by our children. All of our children passed the required end-of-grade tests (EOGs) mandated by the state.

Making the best use of money is a real challenge for charter schools. Because the charter laws do not provide funds for capital items, obtaining that financing is one of the most critical things a new school must do to help ensure success. Imagine being given a budget for operating your home but no funds to buy, furnish, or remodel it. Regardless, the challenge is worth meeting; there is nothing more rewarding than to see a program work, and to see children who may not have done well in a traditional public school blossom.

We learned that building relationships, large and small, can pay big dividends. Most of our successes came from the fruit that was born by a bridge built along the way. After the first year had ended and we had moved out of Atkins, I went to visit Sterling Garris, the principal. He was very complimentary about the shared experience and what having us there brought to his school, and he indicated he and his staff would miss our group. I invited Sterling to come and see our new school and mentioned to him that completing our building would likely take us right down to the first day of school. He replied, "Hey, if you need to open here while you finish your building, just call." Two grown men hugged and parted with high regard for one another. I can truly say the seven years I have spent involved with this project provided some of the most rewarding experiences of my life and brought me in touch with the most unselfish, caring, and dedicated people I have ever met.

"We learned that building relationships, large and small, can pay big dividends."

I will close with a testimonial from a parent who is now a board member. Gayle Anderson is the president of the Greater Winston-Salem Chamber of Commerce. She came to our board during some of our most challenging days and was a valuable asset in helping get the school started. Gayle has been working with a local immigrant family from Mexico for several years, assisting the children as they began their educational experience in the United States. She saw firsthand the challenges these children were having in a traditional public school and became interested in our program. Here is Gayle's story:

ABES has changed the future for the children I volunteer with. Their experience at a traditional public school was difficult. The teachers did not seem to know them as individuals and were not helpful in allowing me to assist them with their homework. My children are ESL, and they needed more assistance and encouragement from a caring staff. Karla and Rigo both entered third grade at ABES at least one grade behind where they should have been. In addition, Rigo has an audio-processing disability which requires teachers to interact with him in very specific ways, creating opportunities for him to learn kinesthetically. Through the unique method of teaching through the arts, Karla completely caught up with the rest of the third-grade class and passed both the language and math EOGs (end of grade tests). Rigo passed the math EOG, something he never could have dreamed of passing a year ago. His disability makes his language performance more difficult, but he has improved dramatically in language arts his first year (because of his language audio-processing disability, Rigo was not required to take the language EOG). He went from hating school and hating math to loving ABES and truly believing he is the "King of Math."

Carlos entered kindergarten at ABES speaking almost no English. At the end of his first year, he is as fluent in English as his non-Spanish- speaking classmates, and he can read. His teacher says he is completely ready for first grade.

"When I get up to sharpen my pencil, no one yells at me."

All three children love going to school, and they are upset when ABES is on a holiday. But perhaps their experience is best summed up in a conversation I had with Rigo after he'd been at ABES for about a month. I asked him what he liked best about his new school. His answer was, "When I get up to sharpen my pencil, no one yells at me." To me, that says it all. A child cannot learn in an environment where he is afraid, and Rigo has thrived in the ABES environment. This is what this project is truly about; changing the future of these and our other children is an investment that cannot be measured, as the rewards can be infinite!

Chapter 6

From ABES to ABS

Robin Hollis' daughter was about to enter kindergarten when her family moved from Boston to Winston Salem, North Carolina, following her doctor husband to a position at Wake Forest Medical School. Hollis saw an ad in the local newspaper about a new type of school opening up, and she was immediately intrigued. As a former elementary teacher herself, she already had a pretty good idea of how a school "could be."

The Arts-Based Elementary School looked to have the potential for that vision. Hollis and her husband decided to take a chance on this charter and enrolled their daughter, Sophie, as one of the sixty-eight original students of ABES. This was the very first year for the school, back when they were no more than five classrooms leased in a vacant wing of one of the district's older middle schools on an impoverished side of the town.

"Talk about being at the right place at the right time . . . "

When Hollis enrolled her daughter, she was quick to let the Arts-Based Elementary School personnel know that she was there to help in any way they needed her. Talk about being at the right place at the right time, Hollis already had a school administrator license, and after a semester of serving as a parent volunteer and then curriculum coordinator, became the new principal of the new school, a position she has held since the school's inception almost two decades ago.

The Arts-Based Elementary School became the Arts Based School in 2013 when they picked up a middle school and dropped the letter "E" from their name (although it is still pronounced the same). "It became like a third child for us," her husband commented regarding their journey with ABS. Both their daughter and son went through their entire elementary and middle school

57

experience at ABS and are now both successfully graduating from Wake Forest University, an elite institution for which ABS prepared them beautifully.

Today, ABS serves 520 students from 21 different zip codes with long waiting lists at every grade level. Their success stems largely from a rock solid commitment to the mission that has never wavered: "The Arts Based School is committed to active and creative scholarly exploration that engages students, their family/community and all school personnel in the learning experience. A strong core curriculum that builds on students' life experiences and multiple ways of knowing/learning will be realized through individualized and intimate integrated interdisciplinary, arts-based instruction."

"'It became like a third child for us,' her husband commented regarding their journey with ABS."

As principal, Hollis is viewed (and views herself) as the instructional leader for both students and staff and is committed to keeping the culture they have created focused on teaching and learning as a collaborative community. The child-focused culture is evident in everything they do, from the way they look at children and adults in the school community to the way they deal with the accountability required by the state of North Carolina. "It's the ABS way!"

It is actually common to see Hollis teaching in the classrooms herself. Over the years, in honor of each staff member's birthday, Hollis gives them a half day off, and she takes over their duties without their having to deduct personal time or requiring a substitute teacher. "I consider it a gift to the teacher, but also a gift to myself," she said.

One year, there were twenty students on the waiting list for second grade, and there was even an available classroom, just not a teacher to teach the class. So they hired an assistant teacher to help cover lunch, recess, and specials, and the rest of the time, Hollis taught the students herself. She says this always helps her more fully understand what she is asking her teachers to do each day in their classrooms.

"The culture we have built here is here to stay. It's 'the ABS way.'"

The teachers clearly respect and admire Hollis. When asked what she looks for in hiring new teachers, it was pointed out that there has been very little teacher turnover since the school's inception. "I have the BEST teachers! I put in the time and attention to those teachers so I can have a better teacher, not to fill out a document of some kind showing they are qualified. It's a different mind-set." She added, "The culture we have built here is here to stay. It's 'the ABS way.'" When asked specifically what was "the ABS way," she elaborated:

We start with the whole child as an individual and create policy that supports the culture we want. For example, if a student asks if they can go to the office, teachers let them go to the office. It's not an accident that we let anyone come to the office anytime. We feel that if a student just needs a break or a walk down the hall or to check in with me or someone in the office, they have a good reason for it, and we honor their judgement. Here's another; homework—we— don't give it. We all read the book *The Homework Myth* by Alfie Kohn and did a book study together and decided there would be no homework here. Even in middle school. If a parent insists on a school giving homework, there are plenty of other schools around that will give it. We don't. I use principal discretion in *everything*! There is no "zero tolerance." We take every issue as it arises and ask, "What should we do in *this* situation, with *this* child?" Sometimes we involve the parent, sometimes not. I know every child, every family. I stand at the door and greet kids every morning and welcome them. We know our students and our culture. If a new teacher is not quite fitting yet, it's not uncommon to hear a staff members say, "She doesn't quite have the ABS way yet but she's getting there."

When asked about awards or scores or recognition for ABS, Hollis replied:

We are usually a "B" school, but we're fine with that because have we philosophical differences with the state. Take, for example, the teaching (and testing) of Reading. The state requires class testing and some of the subtests include nonsense words. We are completely against this. We teach kids to read for *real* reasons and those would not include nonsense words. We teach kids to read to learn and understand the world. We call what we do balanced literacy, and it works for all students. We have as many students with disabilities as the traditional schools in the district, but we start with the whole and work toward the smaller parts. On the nonsense words section of the state test, we tell the kids and parents "the score on this part is not the be all and end all."

Our scores really *could* be higher if we taught to the test, but we do not. We are typically above the national norm in reading and math. The only reason that's important is so others will consider teaching the way we do. Top scores are not what our parents are gunning for. Last year we were recognized as an A+ school for arts integration. We are totally not interested in matching a rubric to get an award. We just don't really care about standardized tests or national recognition. We do not go after this strategically at all. We have tremendous diversity yet all of our subgroups are doing OK and they perform similarly with comparison schools. The difference is, our students *love* this school, and they are each confident about their abilities.

And when asked how, specifically, do you teach? Hollis answered this question:

Well, we are not a conservatory, and we aren't strategically preparing future professional artists; more like future audiences for professional artists. We have great teachers here, and we compliment them with arts specialists. So we take these teachers, we add arts integration and positive discipline. We create relationships with the kids so they grow and learn and take risks. That works perfectly through the arts. Experiential teaching like workshops, have to have a culture of working together. You have to have this safe collaboration and we built that here. This is really why we said yes to adding the middle school. We had invested so much in these kids.

So for example, our 7th graders just studied (and produced) the children's opera, *Brundibar.* This opera was reportedly produced 55 times by children in the German concentration camps in the 1940s (before they were ultimately sent to the gas chambers) but it is a sweet folktale with much important history surrounding it. It was a collaborative effort. We combined Drama, Chorus, Language Arts class, Social Studies class. The infrastructure was a little tough (largely due to licensure issues), but we included every student in the grade level in some way. We are not a conservatory, but they each learn to have access to their own creativity here.

"We start with the whole child as an individual and create policy that supports the culture we want."

The school website shows clip after clip of students dancing, acting, singing, drawing, painting, and playing musical instruments. These are not necessarily stand-alone subjects, but are integrated into all aspects of the core curriculum. When asked if there were plans for a high school in the future, Hollis stated emphatically, "We have no interest in adding a high school. The numbers do not make sense for us, and the high schools in this area are already fantastic."

When asked what the biggest difference in being a charter was, Hollis replied:

> The *bureaucracy*! If we have an idea here and we say, "let's do that," then we do it! Ownership is a big piece of it. If it fails, it's your name on it here. As principal, I'm the only one I have to ultimately make it work. Nobody is going to save me if it doesn't work. I love public schools. I attended them, worked in them, but there are many lessons to be learned from charters.

And what does Hollis see as the biggest challenge?

> That would be isolation. We're not connected very well. For many years, we just kept our heads down. We wanted to do what we do well and took the approach that our work is here with *these* students right here in this school. Once

that was well in hand, when I looked out, I saw that many charters were not like us—some wear uniforms, etc. That's just too rigid. We didn't want to get caught up in the politics of charters either. We have had many important public figures visit out school from both sides of the aisle. For example, after Newt Gingrich's wife visited our school with a republican congresswoman, some of my more liberal parents asked me how I could let them come in and read to our students. I told them that "tonight they are going to talk about what a great school they visited today!" We teach our kids to make friends, and we make friends, too, on both sides of the aisle.

"We have so many visitors now from all over the country. Also, we get student teachers and interns from Wake Forest University, High Point, Winston Salem State, and University of North Carolina at Greensboro to name a few."

We have been becoming more connected recently. We have so many visitors now from all over the country. Also, we get student teachers and interns from Wake Forest University, High Point, Winston Salem State, and University of North Carolina at Greensboro to name a few. So with all of these visitors, we had an idea to start a Teacher Academy. We create our own curriculum, and these folks want to see it, so we are starting this type of lab school for them to come and try it out. We are looking for a building for this right now.

When asked what they plan to do when the inevitable happens, when she leaves or retires, they shared that they do have a succession plan. They do have a strategic plan and lately, every time they look at it, they consider what happens when Robin leaves. First, the culture they've built at ABS is there to stay. It is entirely home grown. They presently have an assistant principal who was a teacher there before moving into leadership. Hollis stated:

If I were to walk out, there would be no problem here. I can think of three teachers off the top of my head who have administrative licenses and could step into leadership but don't want to go someplace else. One of those actually did her internship with me years ago. And I run everything by my AP, everything. And we have always had an amazing Board of Directors. We've also always had good relationships with the district. To quote my husband, "we've just always maintained a good bedside manner." The ABS way is foundational here, and ABS will always be in good hands.

"The culture they've built at ABS is there to stay. It is entirely home grown."

Chapter 7

Growing Grass Roots

REV. PHILIP LANCE, CAMINO NUEVO CHARTER SCHOOL

Philip Lance, a co-founder of Camino Nuevo Charter Academy and chairman of the board of directors, is a nationally recognized leader in the field of community development. In addition to his responsibilities at the school, he serves as the president and executive director of Pueblo Nuevo Development, a nonprofit community development corporation dedicated to serving the residents of the MacArthur Park neighborhood, one of the poorest and most densely populated neighborhoods in Los Angeles. He has a bachelor's degree from Wheaton College in Illinois and a Master of Divinity degree from the General Theological Seminary. He began his career as a minister in the Episcopal Church. Lance has extensive experience and training in community organizing, fund raising, and nonprofit management. While remaining hands-on with both Camino Nuevo and Pueblo Nuevo, he is constantly in search of new ideas and new projects. A school-linked health clinic opened in Fall 2003 and a preschool and high school in Fall 2004.

Several years ago I overheard a friend of mine introduce herself as a "producer." I tried to hide my shock and skepticism. My friend did not fit my mental image of a Hollywood producer. Since then, I have met several more very normal people, many of them relatively of low income, who called themselves producers. In Los Angeles, being a producer is a role rather than an accomplishment. Producers don't have to have money or artistic talent. They use other people's. What they need is a good idea and strong sales skills to convince people to contribute their money and talent to making the idea a reality. In this sense of the word you could say that I am the producer of

Camino Nuevo Charter Academy. Although I produced a school, I wasn't an educator or a financier. I am a community developer. Creating a school was part of a larger strategy to renew a neighborhood.

Producing the school took about eight months. It all began when I stepped down from the podium after winning an award and I met the runners-up, Kevin Swed and Jonathon Williams, cofounders of the Accelerated Charter School. This was in April 1998, and I had never heard of a charter school. I was getting an award from a business organization associate with the University of Southern California. The Entrepreneur of the Decade Award (Social Consciousness category) was for my work founding Pueblo Nuevo Enterprises, a worker-owned janitorial cooperative.

"In my acceptance speech I said that for-profit corporations . . . could do infinitely more for low-income neighborhoods than nonprofit corporations could . . . . Now I would say that the judges should have given the award to the Accelerated School that went on to be name *Time* magazine's school of the year . . . "

In my acceptance speech, I said that for-profit corporations like my janitorial company could do infinitely more for low-income neighborhoods than nonprofit corporations could. Profit-making businesses have the potential to create tremendous wealth that can employ hundreds and even thousands of people. If the business is community-owned and controlled, the potential for sharing the wealth in a way that dramatically impacts a community is even greater. Now I would say that the judge should have given the award to the Accelerated School that went on to be named *Time* magazine's school of the year in May 2001. Meanwhile my janitorial company was still struggling to pay a living wage to forty-five janitors. More than half of the janitors were shareholders of the company, but they were still numbered among the tens of thousands of working poor in Los Angeles. Working long, hard hours day after day, year after year, does not necessarily mean that you make enough money to escape from poverty.

Although I didn't know it at the time, the seed for Camino Nuevo Charter Academy was planted that evening. As the executive director of a community development corporation, I was always looking for new ways to improve our neighborhood. Our mission is to serve the residents of the MacArthur Park neighborhood by creating self-reliant community-based organizations that offer opportunities for economic, educational, and spiritual empowerment. The charter school idea seemed to fit with this mission.

In the weeks following that encounter with the Accelerated Charter School founders, I learned more about charter schools. It occurred to me that they could make great community development vehicles. A charter school in our neighborhood would be a community-based organization that would be financially self-reliant through state funding based on average daily attendance. It would be empowering not only to the students but also to those of us who organized the school. It would give us influence over a larger neighborhood constituency of students and parents. And it would have the potential to strengthen our economic power.

I had been looking for another project to develop and was restless because of a failed effort to start a small swap-meet-style retail incubator in an adjacent warehouse. I wasn't happy when I didn't have something new cooking. In the past seven years, I had founded four organizations in the neighborhood, each one designed to meet a particular need. These included an Episcopal Church congregation (I am an ordained Episcopal minister), a charitable thrift store, a nonprofit community development corporation, and a worker-owned janitorial company.

The intention behind the smorgasbord of neighborhood organizations was to rebuild a blighted area of the city from the grass roots, beginning with a faith-based vision of community and development businesses and businesslike organizations that could attract resources and wealth. I wanted to avoid a social service model of community development whereby we became dependent on nonstop fund raising or government grants. Organizations that depend entirely on outside funding cannot create the "we are the masters of our own destiny" kind of empowered community that I envisioned. Likewise, organizations that provide services through government grants typically become quasigovernmental bureaucracies that keep leaders and clients vulnerable to external political agendas, restrictions, regulations, and overwhelming reporting burdens.

I began my work in the neighborhood in January 1992. This was about four months before the civil disturbances that destroyed hundreds of businesses in the south Los Angeles, Pico Union, and MacArthur Park neighborhoods. The slow economy and burgeoning immigration from Central America during the late 1980s and early 1990s had created a labor glut that kept wages down and unemployment up. Racial tensions were high, and all of the other social problems that come with poverty were increasing.

The neighborhood where I decided to focus my efforts was one of the poorest and most densely populated areas of the city. Ten blocks west of the downtown high-rise business district, the MacArthur Park neighborhood was one of the city's front doors for refugees fleeing Mexican poverty and Central American war. The housing stock was mostly tiny apartment units in large, run-down buildings that were built decades before the city required open space and landscaping. Plummeting real estate prices meant that owners had no incentive to take care of their properties. A building with fifty units could easily have fifty children with no place to play except the hallways.

The large firms and corporations that occupied the office buildings along the Wilshire corridor abandoned the neighborhood because of safety fears and general blight. They left behind vacant shells of buildings. Some of the ground-floor spaces were leased to mom and pop businesses serving the local population, including "envois a Guatemala" (package shipping to Guatemala), immigration services, tax preparation services, Pentecostal churches, and botanicas (providing herbal, self-help remedies rooted in the folk religions of Latin America).

My community organizing effort began with a computerized list—courtesy of the Justice for Janitors union organizing campaign—of janitors who lived in the MacArthur Park zip code area. Using an organizing strategy that I had learned from my years of working with the Industrial Areas Foundation (the organization founded by Saul Alinsky in Chicago in the 1950s), I began to conduct one-on-one meetings with as many of these janitors as possible. I called the janitors on the phone, told them that I was an Episcopalian minister, and asked to meet them to talk about the neighborhood. I met most of them in their home, but some of them felt more comfortable coming to the local diocesan office or meeting at El Pulgarcito (The Little Place) restaurant on the corner of Wilshire and Westlake, where we ate pupusas and pan dulce.

The purpose of these interviews was to begin getting to know the neighborhood and the residents—their interests, issues, hopes, and dreams. I wanted to find potential leaders and potential followers for my proposed congregational development plans. Finally, I wanted to see what kind of grassroots support I could muster for founding a church that would be a true liberating force in the neighborhood on all levels.

By June 1992, I was meeting with a small group of people on Sunday afternoons for a "mass in the grass" in MacArthur Park. Five months later, we opened a thrift store staffed by volunteers from the congregation and supplied by donors from All Saints Church in Beverly Hills. Profits from the thrift store were sufficient to rent an adjacent store that we transformed into a chapel. In July 1993, we incorporated a nonprofit community development corporation called Pueblo Nuevo Development (that became my full-time employer in 1998), and in March 1994 we incorporated Pueblo Nuevo Enterprises, the worker-owned janitorial corporation (for profit).

By 1998, when I discovered the charter school concept at the awards banquet, I had been working in the neighborhood for six years. I had become more and more worried about the future of the children in our neighborhood. For one thing, they weren't learning English well. One day I was visiting with a mother from the congregation for pastoral reasons. I was seated on the sofa of the one-room apartment with her four children gathered around. A ladybug flew through the window and landed on twelve-year-old Esmeralda's arm. I quoted the childhood verse that begins "Ladybug, ladybug, fly away home; your house I on fire and nobody's home." She stared at me blankly. Her mother intervened, explaining that Esmeralda didn't speak much English in spite of spending the past five years in the local school.

The problem was not only that the educational program wasn't working for many children. We also had a major crisis in the district with space for students. Construction of school facilities had not kept pace with the growing population of children. The district had taken two measures to cope: putting students on year-round, multi-track schedules in order to accommodate more students per school, and putting students on buses to remote neighborhoods that had less crowded schools.

"Her son had been threatened with expulsion for discipline problems, and she had never been to her son's school because she didn't have a car . . . . Her boss had granted her a two-hour leave from the sewing factory. . . . I didn't have the heart to tell her it was going to take at least four hours to get to the school and back on the bus."

One day while sitting in the reception area of the local elementary school (unsuccessfully trying to get a meeting with the principal), I witnessed a mother trying to determine how to get to the school where her six-year-old son was bused. Her son had been threatened with expulsion for discipline problems, and she had never been to her son's school because she didn't have a car. The office clerk was trying to explain which streets to take to get to the other school, and the mother was struggling to imagine which bus routes might take her there. Her boss had granted her a two-hour leave from the sewing factory where she worked. I didn't have the heart to tell her that it was going to take her at least four hours to get to the school and back on the bus.

This incident happened not long after the awards banquet where I first hear about charter schools. I began telling my board members and staff about my interest in developing a charter school, and I set up meetings with the few educators that I knew, including the head of the Commission on Schools for the Episcopal Diocese of Los Angeles. She told me to talk to a man named Paul Cummins. After meeting with Paul, doors began to open.

Paul Cummins is the founder of the Crossroads School in Santa Monica, a private school that has won wide acclaim for its humane, joyful, and artistic approach to educating children. Paul is also the founder of several other educational institutions in Santa Monica, including the New Roads School, a younger cousin of Crossroads. Paul was intrigued by the possibility that a charter school could bring a Crossroads and New Roads quality of education to inner-city children who could not afford to pay tuition. By the end of our first meeting, he had agreed to help. At our second meeting, we decided to name the school Camino Nuevo, a parallel name to our respective organizations, New Roads and Pueblo Nuevo.

Paul brought credibility to our plan to start a charter school. His name recognition helped in the fund-raising, and his experience with curriculum helped us to write the charter. He also knew how to imagine school facilities where others saw only neighborhood blight. When I showed him an empty mini-mall across the street from Pueblo Nuevo's thrift store, he assured me that it could be turned into a school. When the chairman of our board asked him how much the renovation would cost, he estimated $200,000. In the final accounting, he was off by $1 million. Our board chair agreed to support the property acquisition because he trusted Paul's renovation estimate. At that time, Pueblo Nuevo Development had $300 in the bank, and the biggest grant we ever got was $30,000 from the Ahmanson Foundation for a thrift store truck. If our board chair had known that the renovation would cost almost $1.2 million, he never would have given the green light.

Another critical component that Paul Cummins brought to the partnership was Bill Siart, a wealthy banker who had founded and led Excellent Education Development (EXED), to help develop and manage charter schools. By Spring 1999, Paul Cummins, EXED, and I were raising money to buy and renovate the mini-mall and writing a charter petition to present to the Los Angeles Unified School District for a K–5 elementary school. We purchased the building in July 1999 for $650,000 cash. The charter was approved by the Board of Education in November 1999. We spent the next eight months raising the $1.2 million needed for the renovation and preparing for opening in August 2000.

We were successful in raising the money because Pueblo Nuevo had an eight-year track record serving the community with its church, thrift store, and janitorial company. Three foundations were impressed enough by this history and our vision for how a charter school could strengthen an impoverished neighborhood that they each gave $150,000 to the campaign. Two years later, two of these foundations gave $750,000 grants toward a middle school building campaign, and the third one gave $300,000.

The school opened in August 2000, immediately winning a number of architectural awards for its unique design. I breathed a sigh of relief feeling that my job was done, but in some ways, the work of creating the school had only just begun. Fortunately, now we had a principal to share the burden. In fact, most of the burden was carried by the principal as I stepped into the background, serving as the chairman of the board of the nonprofit corporation that was incorporated to operate the school.

"All of the rental income serves to strengthen [Pueblo Nuevo Development's] 'bankability,' giving us the financing muscle to embark on new neighborhood development projects."

The partnership between Pueblo Nuevo Development and Camino Nuevo Charter Academy has grown into one that meets Pueblo Nuevo's objectives in many ways. For instance, the school is a tenant that pays $26,000 a month in rent to PND. Some of this rental income covers PND's mortgage on the property, while some of it supports PND's after-school program and wellness center. All of the rental income serves to strengthen PND's "bankability," giving us the financing muscle to embark on new neighborhood development projects.

Chapter 8

Paving the Way to a Brighter Future

Camino Nuevo Charter Academy (CNCA), a network of charters, as we learned in the previous chapter began as part of a grassroots effort to improve the MacArthur Park neighborhood in Los Angeles. Before the first school was founded in 2000, several small businesses were developed in the early 1990s in an effort to help the neighborhood move away from poverty and increase hope for the future of this community.

Rev. Philip Lance, one of the original founders of CNCA, began one of those small businesses, what was called Pueblo Nuevo Development (PND), which managed and handled real estate development in the area including CNCA. The grassroots movement began with Lance's "mass in the grass." Then soon afterward a thrift store and janitorial company were started. Lance saw the importance of changing the future for the children in the area as well as the adults and that naturally led to Camino Nuevo Charter Academy.

"This is the story of how an idea grew to influence so many lives."

From its humble beginnings, Camino Nuevo Charter Academy is now thriving under the direction of Ana Ponce, chief executive officer. Pueblo Nuevo Development is now two separate entities. One is called Grupo Nuevo Los Angeles, which was formed in 2012, the real estate holding company, and Pueblo Nuevo Development and Education Group (PNEDG). Grupo Nuevo Los Angeles became the successor entity to Pueblo Nuevo Development that manages and handles real estate development for our schools.

Both Lance and Ponce are key figures in the growth and development of Camino Nuevo Charter Academy and Grupo Nuevo Los Angeles. Because of these organizations, many children and families have been served. This is the story of how an idea grew to influence so many lives.

Remembering how it all began nearly 25 years ago as a grassroots effort Lance reflected:

> There were no good schools in the area, period, and very few kids were graduating from high school in this area. So I think the main thing we've done for the neighborhood is showing that good schools are possible to have in this neighborhood and that has been an impact, I believe, on the larger school districts, schools in the area. There has been a lot of pressure on the public school system in the last fifteen years to get its act together, and I think a lot of that pressure came from the success of charter schools like ours.

The success of Lance's simple idea, building Camino Nuevo Charter Academy, sparked a number of additional charter schools built under the umbrella of Pueblo Nuevo Development. Lance's plan embodied a philosophy called "industrial areas foundation," which would organize and empower the community by providing financial stability and thereby avoiding a need to depend on constant outside funding. With an estimated 60 million dollars in real estate assets currently, his philosophy was spot on!

Pueblo Nuevo Development began in 1992 and dissolved in 2016 after merging with Grupo Nuevo Los Angeles (GNLA), a nonprofit public benefit corporation which was formed in 2012 and that now holds the real estate properties. In 2016, Pueblo Nuevo Education Development Group (PNEDG) was formed. Its primary function was resource development and capacity building to support the CNCA mission and programs that extend beyond the publicly funded K–12 instruction program, but that are still crucial to the students' early education, academic, college, and lifelong success. With this support, Ana Ponce and the CNCA board direct the operations of the schools.

"There were no good schools in the area, period, and very few kids were graduating from high school in this area."

The Camino Nuevo Charter Academy (CNCA) effort, which started with the opening of one school serving children in grades K–5, has grown to eight schools serving families and children from pre-k through high school. In 2001, soon after opening the original campus in MacArthur Park, CNCA added two middle school campuses to fill a need for increased educational choice in the overcrowded and impoverished area.

In 2004, an early childhood education program opened on the Burlington and Harvard (now called Kayne Siart) campuses, serving two classes of fifteen students each. Expanding quickly to serve 120 students, the Early Childhood Center opened in a separate space in 2005. That same year, Ana Ponce began her role as chief executive officer after joining the organization in 2001.

Camino Nuevo Chapter Academy (CNCA) opened its first high school campus, Camino Nuevo High School, in 2004, and graduated its first senior class in 2008. Now named Miramar High School, the campus serves 400 students in grades 9–12. In 2010, CNCA opened the Jose A. Castellanos K–5 elementary campus as part of Los Angeles Unified School District Public School Choice process.

In 2011, the school's charter was amended to serve students through 8th grade. During the second round of the Public School Choice process, CNCA opened the Sandra Cisneros Learning Academy, a K–8 school in the Echo Park neighborhood of Los Angeles. A second high school, Dalzell Lance High School, was opened in 2014 to accommodate the growing need to serve the student population.

The growth and success of Camino Nuevo Charter Academy has not gone unnoticed. In 2015, Camino Nuevo earned the Bright Spot Award from the White House Initiative on Educational Excellence for Hispanics for closing achievement gaps between English learners and native English speakers. CNCA has gained other accolades including: US News Top High Schools—Gold Award, Silver Award; Top 10 California Charter High School, USC Rossier School of Education Award; California Distinguished Schools Award; California Title 1 Academic Achievement Award; CABE Seal of Excellence Award; Effective Practice Incentive Community (EPIC) Award; and 2016 Gazer Outstanding Achievement in Learning (GOAL) Award, presented by the Advisory Commission on Special Education (ACSE).

Both Philip Lance and Ana Ponce, using very different skill sets yet the same passion and vision, have made their mark on the families of the MacArthur Park Neighborhood and beyond. Now with over 500 well-trained, qualified staff, CNCA provides an opportunity for a brighter future for over 3,600 students in and around the MacArthur Park area. The network has reached beyond the MacArthur Park neighborhood into Echo Park, and Pico-Union (Ponce's family neighborhood).

"Both Philip Lance and Ana Ponce, using very different skill sets yet the same passion and vision, have made their mark on the families of the MacArthur Park Neighborhood and beyond."

Camino Nuevo's mission continues to fall in line with its grassroots beginnings; to prepare students for college as "literate, critical thinkers, and independent problem solvers who are agents of social justice with sensitivity toward the world around them." Camino Nuevo continues to serve impoverished children and families, the majority of whom are immigrants from Mexico and Central America living in the most densely populated areas of Los Angeles. Each school is highlighted in the Table 8.1.

Table 8.1   Camino Nuevo Carter Academy Schools

School	Opening Date	
Camino Nuevo Burlington Campus (K–8—serving 550 students)	2000	Includes a developmental bilingual program to help children achieve academic proficiency in Spanish and English; focusing on the whole child through art, music, dance, drama, and physical education instruction
Early Childhood Center (Pre–K serving 120 children)	2005	Has 5-star quality rating and earned the National Association for the Education of Young Children Accreditation; focus on family engagement
Miramar Campus High School (9–12 serving 400 students)	2008	Preparing low-income, disadvantaged, inner-city youth for success through a rigorous, college-preparatory curriculum that emphasizes real-world projects and a commitment to social justice and community service
Camino Nuevo Kayne Siart (K–8—serving nearly 700 students)	2010	Focuses on learning in a student-centered, experimental learning environment where children with disabilities learn alongside their peers in the classroom; awards include the Grazer Outstanding Achievement in Learning (GOAL) Award, the Bright Spot Award from the White House
Jose A. Castellanos Campus (K–5—serving 510 students)	2010	Offers a developmental bilingual program, a fully inclusive program to support students with disabilities, conceptual math, and authentic literacy programs.
Jane B. Eisner Campus (6–8—serving 270 students)	2012	Offers an integrated learning model within the Humanities block (integrating Reading Workshop/History/Writing Workshop) as well as Conceptual Math and Interactive Science
Dalzell Lance Campus (9–12 serving 450 students)	2014	Preparing low-income, disadvantaged, inner-city youth for success through a rigorous, college-preparatory curriculum that will integrate a STEM approach, real-world projects, community values, and personalization methods. Camino Nuevo High School #2 graduates will go on to become productive members of society

"How did Camino Nuevo grow from its "mass in the grass" beginnings to a successful system of schools that serve over 3,600 children and their families, 96 percent of whom are living in poverty?"

How did Camino Nuevo grow from its "mass in the grass" beginnings to a successful system of schools that serve over 3,600 children and their families, 96 percent of whom are living in poverty? For Lance's part, he brought the vision, the financial know-how and the facilities development expertise to grow Camino Nuevo. As Lance planned his "phasing out" as Executive Director of Pueblo Nuevo Development (PND) and Board President of Camino Nuevo Charter Academy, he shared his perceptions on Camino Nuevo's growth and success. He began at the beginning like a true storyteller. Remembering his vision, to create an empowered community, he recalled:

> The first thing you do when you go into a community is meet a lot of people. Get to know them. Have in-depth conversations with them. Find out where they might fit in and if they are interested in fitting to a vision for doing something together. . . . (And) I'm always kind of listening, what can this person do for my vision. And how can I help them meaningfully become a part of it in a way that is rewarding for them? Then how do I support them as time goes on so that they get what they were expecting in terms of being a part of a project, a vision.

His passion for making a difference in a highly impoverished over-crowded area was only the beginning. He needed to rally others around him, assess what needed to be done, and find the right people to help him make it happen. As Camino Nuevo continues down its path from it grassroots beginning toward paving the way for a brighter future, Lance left us with this thought:

> We all need to learn how to be learners because there is a huge learning curve starting a charter school and it never ends . . . I guess a community of learners, a professional learning community is a phrase we use around here a lot, but that's really important because every day you come up against a new challenge. That you've got to figure out how to handle (each challenge), and all you've got is going back to the books to learn something new to figure out the answer.

While Lance left his mark on the success of CNCA, Ana Ponce, continues to carry the torch. In 2005, early in the charter's history, Ponce joined the staff of Camino Nuevo and later became chief executive officer. With her background and experience, she brought her own passion for changing the future through education for MacArthur Park community. This passion has helped to shape the direction of CNCA and the families it serves.

Ponce, who came to this country as an undocumented, English Language learner at the age of four, beat the odds and became a teacher. In the 1990s, she returned to Los Angeles first as a Teach for America teacher. Later, she joined Camino Nuevo as one its founding teachers. She brought with her the passion and perseverance that only her experiences could shape to propel Camino Nuevo forward. She, along with a devoted staff, continues Lance's vision to empower the families to break the cycle of poverty by opening doors and supporting a community.

Ana Ponce, who grew up in the Pico-Union neighborhood, has the vision Lance shared. She also understands the importance of always learning and moving forward. Her story leads to where Camino Nuevo is today. With Ana Ponce heading its eight schools, Camino Nuevo has made and continues to make a difference for families and children in the greater MacArthur Park Area.

Ponce's childhood prepared her for this important role. The youngest child of seven children, Ponce struggled in school as a non-English-speaking daughter of Mexican immigrants. Expectations from her parents, both of whom spoke no English, were not to attend middle or high school, let alone college. Ponce shared that it wasn't that they didn't care about her, it was what they knew. School was viewed as an unsafe place rather than an opportunity for growth and success.

"Ponce, who came to this country as an undocumented, English Language learner at the age of four, beat the odds and became a teacher . . . . She brought with her the passion and perseverance that only her experiences could shape to propel Camino Nuevo forward."

She battled through difficulties in school, convinced her parents to allow her to continue past middle school, and defied odds by attending Middlebury College in Vermont (across the United States!), and returned home to help families like her own in her childhood neighborhood. Ponce went on to earn her master's degrees from Columbia and UCLA and a doctorate at Loyola Marymount University in Los Angeles. She was named one of the top seven most powerful educators in the world by Forbes Magazine in 2011.

In an interview, Ponce shared these thoughts about her family: "Nothing in my personal experience was done because they didn't love me. It was actually done because they loved me and they cared about me. What they encouraged me to do is what they genuinely thought was the right thing, given their context and their experiences. I value that lesson deeply." She went on to share how proud they are of her.[1]

"She saw her siblings and friends drop out of school to begin working at minimum wage jobs without anyone noticing. She knew there was more to life than this; Ponce wanted to help other families like hers to break the cycle."

Although she was loved and cared for by her family, it didn't change the fact that Ponce was alone and without support as she fought her way through high school (working to pay for her tuition at a private Catholic school) and navigate the world of higher education. She saw her siblings and friends drop out of school to begin working at minimum wage jobs without anyone noticing. She knew there was more to life than this; Ponce wanted to help other families like hers to break the cycle.

"She realizes the difficulties of being a first generation college student through her own experiences. There are many preconceived perceptions to battle, barriers to surpass, and supports to provide."

Ponce understands that families, while they want to do what they understand to be the best for their children, still share some of the same beliefs her family had about school. She realizes the difficulties of being a first-generation college student through her own experiences. There are many preconceived perceptions to battle, barriers to surpass, and supports to provide. Providing a safe, challenging Pre-K school experience is just a piece of the solution. Serving and partnering with the families and community is the only way children can be built up to realize their full potential.

"College Ready, College Bound."

Today, Ana and her staff are working to change the rhetoric by living and supporting what Ponce calls a "simple, but challenging" motto, "College Ready, College Bound." Before Camino Nuevo, this was an area where very few children were graduating from high school let alone attending college; the data looks very different now. With a high school graduation rate for both campuses of 99 percent, there is a greater focus on life beyond high school.

In 2017, Ponce shared, "Our graduates were accepted to nineteen California State University campuses, nine University of California schools, and over sixty private colleges and universities across the country!" According to California Department of Education School Accountability (CDESA), 98.1 percent of the population is listed as socioeconomically disadvantaged for the Dalzell Lance campus and 95.8 percent for the Miramar Campus, and the percentage of Hispanic or Latino population is in the high 90s. Despite the obstacles poverty brings with it to this community, the statistics show that Camino Nuevo is having a huge impact on one of the poorest communities in Los Angeles.

"Understanding her own struggles and the low percentage of students from low-income families that actually complete a four-year college program, Ponce saw the need to add a student and family services coordinator at each school in order to extend the school's supports to Camino Nuevo families."

Even though the statistics looks great, Ana is not complacent in the success Camino Nuevo has experienced. She is passionate about continuing to improve the support system for students and families. Understanding her own struggles and the low percentage of students from low-income families that actually complete a four-year college program, Ponce saw the need to add a student and family services coordinator at each school in order to extend the school's supports to Camino Nuevo families. Camino Nuevo also has a college success team that offers mentoring and guidance to their graduates in college.

Recently, Ana Ponce shared these thoughts:

> We must stay engaged in spaces where we can influence the context we live in and strive to live in. As such, I am especially grateful that today, we as an entire Camino Nuevo community can come together and engage in this thoughtful and inspirational day to learn from each other and to grow with each other.
>
> Now more than ever, we need to prepare for our future and the future of our organization - Camino Nuevo Charter Academy. We opened our doors to about 350 K–5 students back in August of 2000. Today we serve over 3,600 PreK–12th grade students across 8 campuses and over 500 alumni navigating the higher education labyrinth. We have come a long way. Over the last 16 years, we have grown significantly and expanded services—with good results.

- Expansion of our mental health program
- Expansion of our EXL program
- Restructuring of our AP program
- Robust arts education
- Expanded intervention programs
- Dynamic blended inclusion
- Emerging Ethnic Studies program
- Restorative justice approach
- Mindfulness curriculum

We have had impressive results relative to neighborhood schools;

- High School Graduation rate consistently over 95 percent, compared to an LAUSD rate of 73 percent
- 4-year college acceptance rate around 80 percent
- 98 percent of our students graduate meeting the California A-G requirements compared to 53 percent of LAUSD grads[2]

Celebrating the achievements and success of Camino Nuevo Charter Academy, Ponce reminded her audience of the ongoing work that still needs to be done. She continues to forge ahead, continuing the grassroots effort, Rev. Philip Lance started so many years ago.

And we have aspirational goals that reflect our belief in what is possible for our students:

> By 2022, 2,000 CNCA graduates are equipped with the skills, knowledge, and worldview necessary to be literate, critical thinkers and independent problem solvers. As a result of this success, 90% have been accepted to, 80% have attended and 60% have graduated from a 4-year college within 6 years.[3]

Camino Nuevo Charter Academy is truly paving the way to a brighter future for many. The passion, devotion, and perseverance of both Lance and Ponce are a testament to the difference that can be made when a vision is realized.

NOTES

1. Ana Ponce, "The Pride of Pico Union," February 28, 2018. https://www.broadcenter.org/blog/leadership-lessons-ana-ponce/.
2. Ana Ponce, "2017 Success Conference Speech."
3. Ana Ponce, "2017 Success Conference Speech."

Chapter 9

Franklin's Three Pillars

The Foundation for Good Citizens

Franklin Academy prides itself on its commitment to preparing children to be good citizens by providing a traditional curriculum delivered by well-trained teachers. Currently the charter is located on three separate campuses serving K–2, 3–8, and 9–12 grade levels, in Wake Forest, North Carolina. Over 1,700 students currently attend the three schools with typically hundreds of children on a wait list for every grade level. (There are generally around 500 on the wait list for kindergarten every year.)

The not-so secret to its success according to its employees and constituents is in the ongoing commitment to the school's mission, a statement first written over twenty years ago. Although tweaked somewhat over the past two decades, the mission remains true to the founders' original intention: "The mission of the Franklin Academy is to provide an environment that fosters and encourages high standards of academic achievement, creativity, technological sophistication, the love of learning, accountability, self-esteem, and the development of good citizens. Through exceptional instruction, by highly skilled, qualified, and devoted teachers, the highest possible student outcomes will be achieved."

Mr. Robert L. Luddy (Bob), a prominent businessman and philanthropist, wrote the charter for Franklin Academy believing that he could make a difference in the quality of the education options for children in the area. Twenty years later, Luddy and five of the original board members continue to be heavily involved in the popular school. Based on their retention of staff and unusually high demand for student spots in the school over time, Franklin Academy is clearly a place where students and teachers want to come and stay.

Opening its doors in 1998 in a small building with two grades each of K–1 students on a single campus, the school quickly grew. Because of the almost instant rise in demand, another building was added to the first on that same campus. The following year, the two buildings on Franklin Street held two classes each of kindergarten through fifth grade students with a total of 160 children. In addition to eight new classrooms, the new building included an art room, a computer lab, a library, and a gymnasium.

"Through exceptional instruction, by highly skilled, qualified and devoted teachers, the highest possible student outcomes will be achieved."

Luddy's original idea was that children needed a more traditional curriculum. He opened the school based on three pillars, the "Three D's": direct instruction, dress code, and discipline. These pillars or principles, along with the values Luddy believed, make America a great nation: virtuous leadership, well-developed character, and strong work ethic are the foundation for Franklin Academy.

Luddy's "Three D's" began with the elementary school in mind. Direct instruction is the first D, representing the first pillar. Luddy believed that direct instruction with mastery learning at the core was the best instructional approach to ensure student success. The curriculum at Franklin is rigorous with high standards set; the students are taught by well-trained teachers using their research-based method and high expectations are maintained through the direct instruction approach. As students move into middle and high school, the rigor continues with college preparatory coursework, leadership training, and a focus on service learning.

The second D, dress code, applies from Kindergarten through 12 grade. Luddy believed a common dress code would "bolster self-discipline, equality, modesty, and a sense of purpose associated with academics." The third D, discipline, is associated with good citizenship, "Be kind, be responsible, be respectful, be your best." This is their motto.

With Luddy's "Three D's" and the clear mission and vision in place for Franklin, the applications continued to pour in, typically over a thousand each year. In 2002, a middle school was built. There would now be four classes of each grade level, but the configuration changed. The original campus became a K–2 campus and the middle school would house grades 3–8. In this new building, Franklin Academy added twenty-two new classrooms, a media center, a science lab, and a large gymnasium. Two years later a high school was added, and then in 2013 the high school expanded.

Even with the great expansion of the school, Franklin Academy continues to have a wait list as long as the attendance list! That may have something to do with the strong, continuing commitment to Luddy's original mission.

Denise Kent, Head Administrator, shared her thoughts on what makes Franklin Academy so popular. Kent says, "It's all about the mission!"

Kent, like all administrators at Franklin, began as a teacher in the school. In the early years of the charter, she started teaching in a fifth grade class after gaining some prior experience in a Title I school in a nearby district. Kent has since gone on to earn her principal's license and a degree in Special Education. She works very closely with the members of the Board of Directors who are very involved in the oversight of the school.

Under the leadership of Kent, support from the site administrators at the individual schools (K–2, 3–8, and 9–12), and support from the Board of Directors, the school continues to remain true to its mission. She acts as a rudder for the ever-growing Franklin vessel, always steering it to stay on course.

Denise had come to Franklin in 1999 with three years of experience as a traditional public school teacher. Once aboard at Franklin, she worked as a teacher for two years and then moved into the Head of School role. Of course the school was much smaller then, but she has continued to stay at the helm through the growth. All of the administrators at Franklin were first teachers at the school.

"It's all about the mission!"

While a master's in educational leadership was not a prerequisite for the job, she always felt the need to learn more and improve her skills to best help Franklin move forward, so she got one anyway. She is clearly a lifelong learner, stating, "If I don't know what I'm doing I know how to figure it out. I know how to figure out where to get the information I need."

In addition, Kent is another of those leaders for whom no task is too menial. "You know, I don't mind, cleaning writing off the walls in the bathroom." She is proud of the fact that she wouldn't ask a teacher or any staff member to do anything she hasn't already done or would do herself. She loves to be in the classroom whether it's helping stuff the weekly newsletters into backpacks to go home or teaching a lesson in a classroom.

Like many of the other charter school leaders, Denise has also built a leadership team to help share the growing leadership load. Dave Mahally oversees the day-to-day operation of the high school and is assisted by James Cornhe. Other administrators, including Melissa Loide, assist at other campuses. Denise is more visible at the K–8 level where she ensures that Individualized Education Program (IEP) meetings are all in order and on schedule. She does, however, handle the reports and paperwork for the entire organization.

When asked what her staff would say about her leadership, she claims, "I'm not warm and fuzzy. . . . But I have not lived a sheltered life. This allows me, I think, to lend sympathy and empathy to people in every situation. I'm also opinionated, but I'm organized."

In addition to the instructional leadership and management skills, Denise says that while she is not the overly sentimental type, relationship building skills have been important, and she has always worked very closely with the Board of Directors, keeping them involved as a critical part of the Franklin learning community.

"I'm not warm and fuzzy . . . . But I have not lived a sheltered life. This allows me, I think, to lend sympathy and empathy to people in every situation. I'm also opinionated, but I'm organized."

When asked about the best preparation of future charter school leaders, Denise shared her philosophy by focusing on the importance of being a "hands-on" leader at the organization.

> You cannot delegate everything. I may have been accused of being a micro manager, just a smidge, but there's a point to that. When you delegate everything, you lose control. You lose focus. I want to know what's going on in these rooms because if someone stops me in the hall, I want to be able to say, 'No, I'm sorry, second grade went to a bowling trip today. They were not doing science.' I want to be able to guarantee to the parents, that you know, if your child is in teacher A's class versus teacher B's, were they going to be doing the same activities. They're going to be doing the same field trip. I want to be able to guarantee that. I want the same consistency. I want that efficiency, effectiveness, consistency, across. So I don't like delegating. I don't.

Franklin had been founded in 1998 with a focus on using direct instruction as its primary teaching method and over time, this has not changed. When asked about the primary reason for Franklin's success, Kent shared:

> consistency, definitely consistency. We are kind of old-school here. We don't jump on every curriculum bandwagon that goes by. Since our charter is written that K-5 we (use) . . . a primarily direct instruction curriculum, and (as a) direct instruction type of school, beyond updating additions, we use the same reading book and the same math book we have used since 1998.
>
> I think that allows teachers to develop their craft and be confident and feel like they know what they are doing. Along with that, we recognize that teachers need a lot more than an observation or a walk-through. We have a cadre of coaches at our school including administrators. They go in, and it's primarily just to help the teacher develop their craft.

Professional development at the school goes beyond just coaching teachers to perfect their trade. Franklin provides a variety of supports to its teachers, all of whom believe in the mission and vision created at Franklin Academy.

The mission is at the forefront of every decision, and the actions of the Board of Directors and administration are purposeful, which continually cultivates and sustains the culture of the school. One example of this is how teachers are hired. Kent shared that the process is very involved, well planned, and thoughtful in an effort to get the right people on board.

We recruit the best and want to retain the best and we make sure we monetarily reward them . . . . Having that consistency of a staff is just as important. . . . Kim Miller (a current teacher) has been here as long as I have . . . you know . . . . And we have quite a few teachers like that. We have some new ones too, but I think that gives us a nice mix.

The process for finding the right fit begins with recruiting from local colleges (purposefully targeting more conservative colleges and universities) and attending job fairs. Both seasoned teachers and recent graduates are sought after. It's more about the "right fit" she says. Resumes are not just blindly collected, but a short informal interview takes place on the spot at these fairs.

The impromptu interview includes learning about the applicant, but even more importantly, sharing information about the school and the school's unique culture with prospective teachers. Kent understands that Franklin's mission is not for everyone. After the initial exchange, the recruiting team returns to Franklin to process the information, and with that "eye contact" and "brief interview" fresh in mind, decisions are then made regarding who to call in for a formal interview.

"We are kind of old-school here. We don't jump on every curriculum bandwagon that goes by . . . we (use) . . . a primarily direct instruction curriculum, and (as a) direct instruction type of school, beyond updating additions, we use the same reading book and the same math book we have used since 1998."

A complex and time-consuming interview includes a second visit to Franklin by the applicant to visit the school for a day, ensuring a good match. The interview involves administrators, teachers, and the charter board. Kent described their hiring process as "grueling" but beneficial in the long run. It is all to insure that Franklin Academy is the right fit for everyone. Kent shared her thoughts on why hiring carefully is so important.

Most of the time before we offer a contract, we want them to come out, spend the day at the school. Just want to make sure, especially in K-5, that you want to do direct instruction. You want to do explicit teaching. You know that because this is totally different than what a lot of schools are teaching. . . .and understand that, and realize that, and see what it looks like and what it manifests into. So we'll invite them to come out and spend some time. And then usually we'll offer the contract. Or offer the contract, invite them, and let them make that decision.

Teacher turnover is low, and several of the graduates of Franklin Academy have returned to teach at the school. Kent told us, "We have seven or eight of our teachers here who are actually former students (that) went to school here who have graduated. I think it's a little bit more of a testament of what we can do." It also certainly helps keep the culture deeply set within the organization.

Once teachers are hired and on board, they are coached by those more seasoned colleagues. There is a cadre of almost two dozen teacher coaches on staff. Teachers also coach one another and administrators also coach teachers. Thus, Franklin maintains its goal to retain the method and rigor of curriculum and, most importantly, the culture of the school. An elementary teacher described her experience coaching, "It's very much in accordance with growth and learning and developing a strong teaching style that correlates with the direct instruction." Teachers who move into administration are coached as well.

All administrators at Franklin previously taught there. Kent shared her experience working with a newly appointed K–2 Site Administrator, "I spent every day there, every day. . . . So I'd run over here an hour or two. But every day I'd start my day there and end my day there. Because I knew she needed that training . . . . I wanted to make sure they respected her, and that they knew she knew what she was doing." Thus the school's unique mission drives the culture.

The curriculum goes beyond direct instruction as Luddy explains, "The curriculum . . . includes instruction in basic skills, complex analytic strategies and noncognitive abilities. The operating belief is that teachers can help students develop in different areas, on multiple levels and in many important ways." The expectations are set, the teachers trained, data collected, and students are met at their level and provided rigorous academics in small groups.

"All administrators at Franklin previously taught there."

Kent spoke to the use of data to meet the needs of students, "You know our program K–8 is really data-driven. So every four weeks we sit down and do data meetings, kindergarten through eighth grade. When those kids are not at those points where we need them to be, we put them in remediation. We come back. We look at the data and so we do what we need to do."

As with all charter schools, the admission process is by blind lottery. Kent jokes that their lottery is so blind many of the families that get in have never even toured the school. They want to be there based on the reputation the school has built within the community over time.

The program is developed with the "commitment to build good citizens" with the following goals for its high school students (as outlined in the student handbook):

Outcomes of a Franklin Academy student recognizing the importance of character in becoming a good human being, we pay close attention to the formation of character by instructing and challenging our students to absorb and practice several strengths and virtues through a variety of curricular methods including our own set of supporting standards incorporated into our rigorous curriculum frameworks. As such, we have an exceptional culture of civility, fairness, and respect at Franklin Academy.

By graduation, each of our students will have mastered these fifteen character outcomes implemented through lesson plans and instructional strategies.

1. Self-Reliant
2. Critical Thinker
3. Virtuous Leader with Well-Developed Judgment
4. Continuous Learner
5. Competent Technical Skills
6. Truth Seeker
7. Unfailing Integrity
8. Astute Problem Solver
9. Cooperative and Contributive Team Member
10. Strong Work Ethic
11. Dreams and Aspirations to Change the World
12. Traditional American Values and Entrepreneurialism
13. Well Developed People and Communication Skills
14. Gratitude
15. Healthy Mind, Spirit, and Body

It is not by accident that Franklin Academy is a sought after school for so many. It, like so many charter schools, developed a charter for a specific group of students and has stayed true to its mission for the past twenty-five years. It is a model of a school that remains grounded in its core beliefs, communicates those beliefs, and practices them with intention and meaning. When asked about her greatest accomplishment as head administrator at Franklin, Kent summed up what Franklin Academy is all about:

I think one of the biggest rewards is being able to offer an option for families. You know, we're not utopia for everybody. We are not, and any charter school that thinks they are, they are dead wrong. And any parent that thinks this school is a one size fits all is dead wrong. I mean, we offer an option. There is nothing wrong with Wake County schools. You know, I firmly believe school is what you make it . . . I'm glad that we're able to offer that because we have students here that could not find success elsewhere. And I'm not saying it's the previous school's fault or whatever, I mean, I don't know, I wasn't there. But these children have found success here.

As the head of Franklin, Denise Kent leads with a devotion to the school and commitment to the community. Luddy, the Board of Directors, the administrators, and staff are all passionate about the success of the children and care deeply about the families they serve and about the community in which they live.

"It is a model of a school that remains grounded in its core beliefs, communicates those beliefs, and practices them with intention and meaning."

The overarching goal is to provide a safe, caring, nurturing environment where children come to grow academically, physically, and emotionally. The philosophy and practice of how that is to be accomplished is well planned and implemented with fidelity by a committed group of professionals.

As Kent said, this school is "not utopia for everybody." The goal is not to serve every student, everywhere, but to serve the children and families who believe in the mission and vision of Franklin Academy and choose to be a part of this unique culture. Based on the long-term success and sustained growth of this organization, Franklin Academy is achieving its goals.

Chapter 10

One Family's Quest for
a Better Education

Thomas Jefferson Classical Academy is a K–12 school located in the north western mountains of North Carolina. The school serves approximately 1,300 students and is one of the top performing schools in the state and nation. Over twenty years ago, Thomas Jefferson Classical Academy began as one family's mission to provide a quality education for their five children.

Joe and Georgia Maimone moved from New York to a quiet town in Rutherford County, North Carolina, in the hopes of homeschooling their five children. Joe had earned an MBA from the University of Chicago and was Vice President of Banker's Trust before he and Georgia decided to move south. As they settled in, they met other families who were seeking the same educational options: a quality school in hopes of a successful future for their children.

In 1997, the Maimones were homeschooling their five children using a classical curriculum. As they met other families, questions about schools would come up in conversations. More families became interested in the classical curriculum that the Maimones used in their homeschool setting. Then as fate would have it, North Carolina had just passed legislation to authorize charter schools in the state, Article 14A in 1996, so the timing was perfect.

"As they settled in, they met other families who were seeking the same educational options: a quality school in hopes of a successful future for their children."

These conversations led to action; and a new charter school was born. Joe shared how the concept of the new school started, "So we really started the school with that mind-set that this is an option for homeschooling parents and parents who just want a different college-prep type focus for their kids."

Timing and economics provided good conditions for the concept of this little charter school to grow.

In this same timeframe, the socioeconomic conditions in Rutherford County were changing as textile mills, furniture factories, and family farms began closing down due to competition from foreign sources. Families began to realize that a college education was becoming more essential for future opportunities for their children. The homeschool curriculum, interest from other homeschool families, and the economic turnaround, created an impetus for action.

After hearing interest from other families in late 1997, the Maimones began investigating the requirements and feasibility of starting a charter school in the area. They mobilized the interest group and led the effort of writing a charter to start a new school. In retrospect, the timing for a new college preparatory focused program could not have been better for the community. Joe explained the importance of the need for this new charter school,

> And little did we know that it would blossom into filling a huge niche and need in the community because what we couldn't foresee at the time was within the next five years most of the mills and furniture factories would be shutting down in the area, and a lot of those families that relied on a ninth grade education to go work in the mills or the farms, no longer had that opportunity. They needed more. The discussion and understanding of how important a four-year degree is became a centerpiece of the community along with our school. So, our timing was very fortunate, and [we] filled a great niche and need for the community.

The new school would offer a classical education, which would include E. D. Hirsch's Core Knowledge curriculum as much as possible, and would focus on college preparation. They began attending informational sessions in Raleigh and Charlotte, and began writing the application for Thomas Jefferson Classical Academy. Because the process was so new in the state, there were many unknowns.

"The homeschool curriculum, interest from other homeschool families, and the economic turnaround, created an impetus for action."

The name of the school was carefully chosen to convey three important ideas:

1. **Thomas Jefferson**, the founder of the University of Virginia, was a vocal supporter of a classical education. One of his many quotes on education summarizes well the philosophy of the school, *"A society that wishes to be ignorant and free, in a state of civilization, wants what never was, and never will be."*

2. **Classical** conveys the intent of offering a traditional classical education.
3. **Academy** expresses the message that this will be a serious institution of learning, with a uniform policy that would help ensure that students would not judge each other based on their outer appearance, and that when students put on the uniform, it is time to work!

The mission was clear, the purpose set. The hardest work was yet to come.

In the first year of planning, the Maimones learned all they could about founding and running a charter school, distributed materials about the potential new school, and met with interested families. They also recruited members from the county to assist with the behind the scenes work and to become their first board of directors. At this point, Georgia Maimone became the first board chair, and Joe took the future headmaster role. By-laws were written, plans for curriculum developed, facilities explored, and teachers recruited, all with no compensation.

Clarity of their mission and support from families was not lacking but finding a site for the school was a challenge. The Maimones and their team received preliminary approval of the charter application in November of 1998, and began the process of looking for a school building. The new board sent a request to the local county school board, asking for one of their abandoned school buildings. (According to North Carolina State law, districts must lease unused buildings to charter schools if they are not being used by the district.)

There had been two district school buildings slated for demolition or abandonment that year. The Thomas Jefferson Classical Academy (TJCA) board requested either facility. The process was challenging; however, after some difficulty, they were granted one of the facilities in April of 1999, just four months prior to their scheduled August opening. Challenges of providing a suitable facility for the teachers and students continued.

Unfortunately, this facility was in need of extensive and expensive renovations. Although a $30,000 start-up grant was awarded by the state for renovations, it was not nearly enough to get the building ready for students. A required new boiler alone would cost $30,000! The building also required electrical rewiring throughout. There was asbestos in the annex that had to be removed by a Hazmat team.

The plumbing system was inadequate and would be condemned if they could not tap into the plumbing system of the facility next door. Fortunately, and largely due to the relationship building skills of the leaders, the neighbors agreed to allow the school to tap into their septic system. However, plumbing was not the only issue.

Air conditioning units throughout the building were missing or broken, the walls were damaged with numerous holes, the ceilings were peeling, bathroom doors were rotting, the auditorium chairs were missing hardware and broken, lockers were dented and broken, window blinds were filthy and broken, and the basement, which had been used for classes the previous semester, was so damp that the paint was peeling from the walls. There were no countertops for labs, no equipment, no textbooks, and no money to pay for any of it.

"A society that wishes to be ignorant and free, in a state of civilization, wants what never was, and never will be."

With much work to be done, the Maimones applied for a loan, using their home as collateral, and began, with the help and generosity of many parents, to renovate the building in what seemed an impossible task with just a few months' time to be ready for school. Three parents of prospective students were electricians. They would voluntarily work evening shifts for three months to rewire the entire building.

Weekends were full with parents and prospective students helping to spackle and paint walls, sand floors, scrub and clean lockers, desks and bathrooms, and to repair broken doors and chairs. The Maimones were ever-present working side-by-side with the families and volunteers.

The founding teachers were hired in May of 1999 and most of them volunteered much of their time that summer to help renovate the building. (Those original teachers remain an integral part of the school today.) In addition, Mr. Maimone sent letters to several of his prior co-workers in New York, asking for donations to assist with renovations. In addition, several local Foundations agreed to support their efforts, including the Stonecutter and Tanner Foundations.

In the midst of all of this activity, the Maimones continued to answer phone calls and faxes to recruit students, examine and order textbooks, and hire additional teachers. Thomas Jefferson Classical Academy opened in an acceptable, safe building in August of 1999 with 110 students, a small number of teachers, and with Mr. Maimone as the headmaster.

Because of the interest in college-prep, the charter was originally written for a high school, grades 8 through 12. However, as they were initially surveying the community for school needs, many families had expressed interest in a middle school option; the charter was amended and TJCA was approved for 7th grade that first year and 6th grade the second year. Starting in 1999 with grades 7 through 9, the following year they added grades 6 and 10, then added 11 and 12 in the subsequent years, graduating the first class of high school students in 2003.

In 2005, a concern arose as the teachers realized that students entering in 6th grade were unevenly prepared. Achievement data for these students revealed a gap; students were either ready for a college-prep experience, or they had very limited skills. A decision was made to add classes at the grammar school level. A kindergarten through 5th grade school was added.

This addition of lower grades fit very well with their charter, because they used the Core Knowledge curriculum already. Hirsch had written a series of books, *What Every Fifth Grader Needs to Know, What Every Fourth Grader Needs to Know*, and on down to Kindergarten. Hirsch's Core Knowledge curriculum already matched the school mission and included a spiraling curriculum for grades K through 8.

Also during this time period, Thomas Jefferson Classical Academy partnered with a newly versioned network of schools called Team CFA that used the Core Knowledge curriculum. CFA is an acronym for Challenge Foundation Academy, a philanthropic support organization originally founded in 1988 as a charitable trust to assist with school choice initiatives.

According to their website, after the inception of charter schools in 1991, Team CFA turned its focus toward charter school support. The goal was to support efficient and effective schools with high academic standards. The number of Team CFA charter schools continues to grow; as of this writing there are eighteen public charter school members in the Southeast, Southwest, and Midwestern states in the United States.

Team CFA seeks to promote best practices in K–8 classical education by providing curriculum (the Core Knowledge Sequence), nationally normed testing (Northwest Evaluation Association's Measures of Academic Progress (MAP) test), and other supports, such as coaching, to charter schools. The foundation provides oversight, guidance, and financial support in the form of grants. With the support of Team CFA, the Thomas Jefferson Classical Academy Team CFA grammar school (K–5) was developed and opened on a separate campus in an old building in 2007. TJCA-CFA was approved by the state for the expansion of grades from 6–12 in the original charter, to K–12 after that 2007 year.

"Thomas Jefferson Classical Academy partnered with . . . Team CFA that used the Core Knowledge curriculum . . . . Challenge Foundation Academy, a philanthropic support organization originally founded in 1988 as a charitable trust to assist with school choice initiatives."

Thomas Jefferson Classical Academy had opened in 1999 with 110 students in grades 7, 8, and 9, but by the 2004–05 school year it had grown to roughly 450 students in grades 6 through 12. When the grammar school

(K–5) opened in 2007, it immediately filled to capacity. The demand was very strong—especially with the 6–12 school gaining traction through the success of the graduates who were gaining admission into well-respected colleges with substantial scholarships. Parents were increasingly anxious to jump on board.

The number of students at TJCA-CFA grew from 400 to about 1,100 when the grammar school opened. In fall of 2010 a new school was built with the help of Team CFA to house the grammar school. Since that time, the student population (K–12) has grown to 1,300, limited mainly by facility constraints. The high school has added seven modular classrooms in the last six years just to accommodate the growth. There are now plans to build a new high school building; something that the Maimones have dreamed of!

Although the school has grown from a small, one-campus facility to two larger campuses with 1,300 students and 160 staff members, TJCA-CFA still has a small, close-knit family community feel. As Mr. Maimone walks the halls for both the high school and grammar school, students high-five him as he calls students by name. Teachers share their admiration for Joe (Mr. Maimone) as well, often referring to him as "coach." It may be because of Maimone's perception of his role as a leader:

> I'm just a worker bee, and I just feel like I serve others. My job is to help others. I believe very much in the servant-leader philosophy, where I'm not going to ask teachers to do something I wouldn't do myself, whether that's mopping a floor, or cleaning a toilet, or, you know, helping a child who's crying or upset. I just really believe that I have to show by example as a leader. I think that's helped me in a lot of ways.

He hires individuals based on their belief in the mission of the organization and their expertise, and treats faculty and staff as valued professionals. They, in return, remain true to the school's vision and mission. Joe explains,

> My philosophy is, if you join us, you are going to join a great staff of highly academic, motivated teachers who are professionals, and it's your job to get in that classroom to get together the curriculum and the structure that is going to work best for the students that you have. And I think the teachers over the years have appreciated that feeling of professionalism.

New faculty and staff receive professional development, mentoring, and coaching to stay true to the high standards of rigorous college-prep classical education. When asked what his staff might say about his leadership, he diverted the focus to his team and the school's mission. He stated:

I have a lot of faith in the people we have around us, and I realize growing from 12 staff members that very first year to 160 staff members today, that you can't do something like that on your own. I was very fortunate to hire and surround myself very capable and competent people that married into the mission. And I think that's a crucial part of the success. We were able to hire folks who really believe that we were meeting a very important need in this community, not only for college-prep, but also for classical education.

When pressed for words staff might use about his style, he elaborated:

I never yell and get angry at a teacher or a staff member. I've been here 17 years, and I take a lot of pride in, in sitting down and being able to talk through, in a very positive way, good, bad and ugly with staff and teachers. I take a lot of pride in that I have an open-door policy that my staff member are very comfortable talking to me about any situation. They don't have to fear that I'm going to blow up at them or be very angry with them. We'll talk through it, work through problems and issues.

When asked about the state of charter schools going forward Maimone commented:

You know I firmly believe that competition is healthy, some will call it, unhealthy, competition between traditional schools and charter schools. I promise you that an administrative person from Rutherford County Schools will never tell you this to your face, but the presence of our school has forced the local school systems around us, Cleveland, Rutherford Counties in particular to really take a good hard look at how well they are serving their customers. It's forced them to be more customer-driven for the parents and students because they see students leaving to come to us.

When asked about preparing charter school leaders, he emphasized the importance of motivation and staying motivated over the long haul. "To me, a leader, not only has to motivate himself, but has to know how motivate, or figure out how to motivate all those around him or her to do the best job that they can to leave that legacy of why you are doing this in the first place."

Maimone's philosophy is clearly working for the students of TJCA. TJCA was ranked by *Newsweek Magazine* and the *Washington Post* as one of America's Best High Schools. In 2017, US News Best High School Ranking listed TJCA as 135th in the nation, 5th in North Carolina, and 47th for all charters nationally. The school is also recognized as a Core Knowledge School of Distinction by the CK Foundation in Charlottesville, Virginia. This led to TJCA-CFA becoming recognized as an Honor School of Excellence in North Carolina.

Since the school's first graduating class in 2003, the average SAT scores of graduating seniors rank consistently near the top of the state and 100 percent of seniors who apply to four year colleges are accepted. Each year, over 95 percent of graduates go on to four-year colleges.

TJCA was ranked by *Newsweek Magazine* and the *Washington Post* as one of America's Best High Schools.

With a focus on rigorous student achievement and the school's growth over almost two decades, Maimone, his team, and the families still maintain that collaborative family-like community that the Maimones envisioned when they began this journey. When Joe reflected on the past twenty years as the founding Headmaster of Thomas Jefferson Classical Academy, he shared:

> It's been a journey, that's for sure. . . . It's one of those things that if I had known 20 years ago how hard this job would be, I would have been scared to death and probably wouldn't have followed through with it. And yet, the gratification from the positives, the success of the students and the outcomes of the students are well worth every bit of . . . energy that has been expended. And I just hope and pray that I can keep that fire going. That's the challenge. How do I keep motivating myself to motivate others?

As TJCA-CFA continues to serve the rural population in the mountains of Rutherford County, North Carolina, the Maimones can see the fruits of their labor. The website is a reminder of who TJCA-CFA is, the pride of its community. The home page of the site features a graduation cake with a photo of the 2017 graduating class and the names of their future colleges framing the photo.

Clicking through the website you can find testimonials from students, families, and community members who share their gratitude for their experiences and their success stories. Some of the comments reflect on the academic achievement, while others highlight the collaborative family-like community:

> The TJCA students worked hard from the time they stepped off the bus until the day was done. They did everything that was asked of them, and then some. Your students were not afraid to get their hands dirty and got the job done. It was a pleasure to be around them and see how hard they worked and how excited they were with the project. (President, Shelby Civitan Club, Cleveland County Board of Education)
>
> I hope your and the rest of TJ's school year has been going smoothly. I wanted to write this e-mail to thank you and the entire faculty and staff of Thomas Jefferson Classical Academy for providing such a quality education.

While I realized that TJ was a good school while enrolled, I can only now begin to see the true extent of what an amazing academic environment it was. My first few weeks of classes at North Carolina State University have gone exceedingly well, and connections between my current classes and previous classes at TJ are seamless. (Class of 2016 Alumnus)

Good morning Mr. Maimone: I wanted to pass along a quick note from a proud parent about my daughter Haley (2012 TJCA Grad). Haley is set to graduate from Baylor University this May with her B.S. in Biology (minor in Religion) Magna Cum Laude. Additionally, we have just learned within the past week, that she has also been accepted into membership in Phi Beta Kappa—as good as it gets in the world of Honor Societies!

I know how proud you are of TJCA graduates, so I simply wanted to add this information to your file! It is yet another example of the great impact that TJCA makes in the lives of its students. Thanks for allowing me to share this good news with you. (Parent of 2012 Graduate)

"As TJCA-CFA continues to serve the rural population in the mountains of Rutherford County, North Carolina, the Maimones can see the fruits of their labor . . . . TJCA-CFA is, the pride of its community."

When the Maimones and teachers talk about TJCA-CFA, it's not about any one individual; it's about the students and the community they have worked to build. The Maimones moved to the mountains of North Carolina in hopes of providing a safe family-focused education for their five children in the early 1990s; they and their TJCA-CFA team have influenced a much larger "family."

Chapter 11

Living the Mission and Vision

David Machado moved with his parents to Lincolnton, North Carolina, from the northeastern United States while he was a teen in high school. He then earned a college degree in business administration from Western Carolina University and later joined his father in the tire business in Lincolnton. He was and still describes himself as a businessman. He was never involved in education beyond just being a student. However, things changed for him shortly after charter schools started to become part of the landscape of North Carolina.

After joining his father's business, David got married and started a family. His precious daughter was a shy little girl who, along with most of the local children, attended the nearby elementary school in their small town. He was happy with the school and his daughter's education when a new school came upon the landscape. His daughter seemed content and was learning. Life was good.

His wife started talking about moving their daughter to the new charter school during the infancy of charters in North Carolina, and naturally, he was reluctant. Regardless, his wife moved on with her decision to try out the new Lincoln Charter School, and Machado, not wanting to leave the success of the school and his daughter's education to chance, joined the board of this school in its second year.

Lincoln Charter School obtained its charter in 1998. It was a unique charter in that it requested authorization for two different campus locations in Lincoln County. The original charter called for two K–8 schools on opposite sides of the county that would feed into one centrally located high school. The first year the board opened one K–5 campus in Lincolnton, North Carolina. The following year the board opened a second K–5 campus in Denver, North Carolina, and then each school grew by one grade level per year.

As the separate campus schools grew, it was evident that while the two schools shared a name, each became a unique campus with different specialties. While they both had a rigorous college-prep curriculum and community service focus, one developed a stronger arts program and the other focused more on athletics. The board petitioned the state to alter the charter to remain K–12 on two separate campuses under the direction of a single board.

"The original charter called for two K–8 schools on opposite sides of the county that would feed into one centrally located high school."

The petition was a bit dicey since at the time; North Carolina had a cap of 100 on the number of charter schools in the state and this tactic could be seen as working around that policy. After the approval of Lincoln Charter was approved as one school on two separate campuses, the state changed its regulations to not allow this type of structure, making Lincoln Charter the only charter in the state with this configuration.

While still operating as a single charter with one chief administrator and board of directors, Lincoln Charter is the only North Carolina charter school built on two separate campuses. The cap on the number of charter schools allowed in North Carolina has since been lifted.

Today each campus has three classes per grade level from Kindergarten through grade 5. The two middle schools have four classes per grade level. And the high schools combined have a little more than 150 students per class per grade. Today the school, the largest charter school in North Carolina, serves 1,900 students that come not only from Lincoln County but also from several of the surrounding counties. They consistently have a large waitlist of more than 2,000 students.

Over the past twenty years, Lincoln Charter School has grown into a very successful school, albeit composed of two different campuses, serving the community; Machado's role in the world of charter schools has changed too. When Machado joined the board of directors, he brought with him his business background and his knowledge as a long-time resident in the community. He was soon elected president of the board.

"He was and still describes himself as a businessman. He was never involved in education beyond just being a student."

After serving six years, Machado decided to step down from the board. This same year he sold his business and determined it was time to slow down. However, there was a need for a principal in one of the high schools. The board asked Machado to take the interim position for one year while they looked for a new principal. When Machado told the story of how he began his tenure in charter school administration, he ended with, "And that was fifteen years ago!"

Although he hadn't intended on becoming a long-term school leader, he eventually became chief administrator of Lincoln Charter. When he was interviewed for this book, he was a well-respected leader in the community who was preparing to leave Lincoln Charter School to become North Carolina's top charter school official, Director of North Carolina Office of Charter Schools for the Department of Public Instruction.

From managing his own business to running one of the largest North Carolina charter schools to becoming the state's top charter school official, David Machado credits much of these accomplishments to his business background combined with his ability to surround himself with a team of educational experts. His humility, work ethic, and trust in others played important roles as well.

While serving on the board before taking on the leadership role, Machado remembers a number of principals who came and went, who, while having a background in education, were not ready for the business aspects of running a charter school. During his eleven years directing the school Machado surrounded himself with high-quality educational leaders. He trusted them with the task of instructional leadership always remembering that it was his ultimate responsibility to head the school.

When asked what attributes lead to his success as a leader, he shared, "I think the ability to surround myself with good competent people, giving them authority and empowering them so they are not afraid to make decisions." He added that mistakes are part of growth. Without mistakes, there is no learning. His staff knows that it is ok to make mistakes, fix them, learn from their mistakes, and move on.

Business skills related to finance, budgeting, marketing, and human resources are all securely in Machado's wheelhouse. Charter schools have a unique challenge of doing more with less, because in North Carolina, like most states, charter schools do not receive the same funding as traditional public schools. Effective school leaders need to be creative to assure students and families are provided a quality education.

Machado often used his knowledge, skills, and connections in the community to make sure the school received the best resources available to them. One such example was shared by Machado as he related his efforts to establish a high-quality, low-cost lunch program. He met with a variety of local businesses to find healthy choices at a very reasonable price. Not only did the families get the best the town had to offer, but local merchants benefitted.

These skills are not the only reason behind the school's success. Machado's philosophy is that no job is too small or unimportant. He "walks the talk." His strong work ethic and generous service to the school were second to none. One high school teacher at Lincoln commented on the way Machado exemplified kindness and thoughtfulness; "he would arrive at school every day before the teachers and make the coffee. AND make sure it was cleaned up at the end of the day."

"Mistakes are part of growth. Without mistakes, there is no learning. His staff knows that it is ok to make mistakes, fix them, learn from their mistakes, and move on."

Another teacher shared that he always recognized important personal events in the staffs' lives such as not only sending a card upon the death of a loved one, but sending flowers. She recalled, "I don't even know how he knew where to send them, but he found out!" The staff knew he valued them, just as he expected the staff to value and take care of the students and families. He provided the resources needed to run a school and built a culture of service and caring through his actions.

Machado's business background may be the reason he created a culture where customer service and school pride comes first. He believes that mission and vision must be clearly communicated in the physical and cultural aspects of the school community. He understands that a school needs to be orderly, clean, and conducive to learning.

Machado took pride in the physical aspects of the school. The school logo was displayed proudly throughout the school. Teachers understood that they and their classrooms were the face of the school. Machado understands that choosing a specific school is a family's choice, just as he and his wife chose Lincoln Charter for his daughter. Policies are in place to insure student and family voices are respected.

Both Machado and his teachers shared the belief in the importance of thoughtfully considering families' expectations but never at the expense of the school's mission. Marketing and living that mission were a top priority. According to the school's website, its mission is "to facilitate the development of college ready individuals through emphasis on rigorous academics and our community expectations: honesty, respect, empathy, responsibility, service and preparedness."

"The staff knew he valued them, just as he expected the staff to value and take care of the students and families."

Observing the school, facilities, staff, and students and speaking with Machado, the focus is clearly on student achievement. He shared stories of college successes, student trips to conferences, and of course, the school's NC Report Card. When asked, what is your biggest reward as a charter school leader, Machado didn't hesitate as he reported, "Number one is seeing my teens graduate or them coming to tell me that they just got accepted to the school they want to attend, and then having them come back after their first semester and telling us that they were prepared for college. And that's almost as good as a paycheck."

Focus on academics for college prep is one part of Lincoln Charter School's mission; service to others is equally as important. The high school has a mandatory service requirement for students. In fact, volunteer service hours are required of students beginning in kindergarten. The requirement for elementary students is five hours, just enough to allow them success without becoming overwhelmed. The amount of service time required grows with the children. High school seniors have a 50-hour commitment.

As one of the teachers shared, the students take service very seriously. They are involved in activities directed by the school, like the annual Veteran's Day breakfast, or self-directed, like volunteering at the Special Olympics. Each year the students, on their day off of classes for Veteran's Day holiday, come together to make breakfast for any and all veterans in the area. It is a highlight of the year for the school and community.

The expectation that all students participate in service for others starting in kindergarten sets the culture of kindness and caring for others, a culture that Machado modeled.

"Number one is seeing my teens graduate or them coming to tell me that they just got accepted to the school they want to attend, and then having them come back after their first semester and telling us that they were prepared for college. And that's almost as good as a paycheck."

Lincoln Charter School is now in its nineteenth year, and David Machado has moved on to serve the charter profession at the state level in North Carolina. Jonathan Bryant has stepped in to replace Machado as Chief Administrator at Lincoln Charter. He is no stranger to the school, having served as Assistant Chief Administrator for a number of years. Also, he had already worked at the school for eight years at the time of his appointment. Not surprisingly, Bryant has a BA in Economics and an MA in Educational Leadership. He has the background in business like his predecessor and preparation in education leadership as well as experience in the community.

The school continues to thrive under Bryant's leadership. In 2015, the Lincolnton campus built a new school structure. The beautiful building, surrounded by athletic fields and playgrounds, highlighted the school's mission. The walls displayed the actual mission statement of the school in the office.

The halls leading from the office toward the classroom were lined with each graduating senior's name and a list of his or her college acceptances followed the student's name. The number one choice was written at the top. Even in the elementary school area, school spirit supporting the college prep culture of the school was apparent; the hallways, much like streets, were named after colleges. This year, a new building is being added to the Denver campus. The largest charter school in North Carolina continues to grow.

Academically, Lincoln Charter School continues to out-perform schools around it. It consistently outperforms the state scores earning a School Report Card grade of B and meeting or exceeding growth. But as Mr. Bryant's welcome message on the website says, "until you actually visit LCS, until you talk with members of the faculty and staff, until you see the faces of the children in the classrooms; you will not truly appreciate all that Lincoln Charter School has to offer." Mission, school spirit, and service to others continue to serve the students well at Lincoln Charter School.

Conclusion

A Journey Forward

What do these case studies in leadership and charter school development depict? What can others learn from these schools, these leaders? Each leader's narrative revealed unique journeys with different paths taken, different choices made; however, the narratives shared some commonalities; these leaders were all entrepreneurs with a passion to create and then guide their schools toward success over the long haul. Each developed a specific mission and vision to improve educational opportunities and a better future for a specific group of children.

While roles changed for these individuals and new team members were added over time, the mission, whatever it was, prevailed as their guiding compass. The leaders used their keen reading of the winds of human and institutional change over time and thoughtfully and tirelessly navigated their respective ships.

Equally consistent to sticking to the mission was the solid commitment of each leader to the organization they had created. Without exception, every leader is still involved at some level in their schools; some as board members and consultants, others continue in their original leadership role. Their unusual long-standing commitment to their communities set them apart from traditional school leaders.

These leaders came to the charter school world with different backgrounds, some from business, others from education, the military, and one as a minister; however, they each felt called through a strong passion, for different reasons, to improve a learning environment for a specific community. They also shared a need to separate and be freed from the traditional public school system, to act on their own beliefs to create their own schools and achieve their goals for their constituents. They listened internally and valued that input over external noise or traditions.

The organizational structure created from their respective state charter school legislation presented them with this opportunity; albeit an opportunity wrought with many challenges, and they pounced on it like the courageous risk-takers that they were. These leaders felt driven, wrote their own scripts, and ventured out to create their schools. The juxtaposition of their singular drive combined with the flexibility of infinite possibilities enticed them into action.

Also unique and perhaps most noteworthy of their stories is that they never left their original constituents. They stayed at their schools. They each created an individual identity through an institution that over time became shared with all involved in the school, including the families and communities in which they existed and they continued to support and steer the effort for nearly a quarter of a century. That is extraordinary dedication.

LESSONS LEARNED

As part of our interview we asked these leaders what lessons they would share with future charter school leaders. We conclude with a summary of their insights. Some of these lessons can arguably be formally taught and learned to some extent, but for them, were mostly developed informally on the job, through experience. Some went back to school themselves to obtain the traditional credential for school leadership, others didn't, but none recommended them as a prerequisite for creating and leading a charter school.

None saw their leadership abilities as innate either. As Doug Thomas from Minnesota New Country School offered, charter leadership can be learned through "both formal and out-of-the-box training, thinking and experimenting and most important, communicating with parents, students and teachers." Education is a people-centric business and people change. Every day in a school is a new adventure to some extent. Consequently, one nonnegotiable component was that these leaders were forced to be lifelong learners. Furthermore, they embraced the role, and none was above learning from their learners themselves.

COMMUNICATING THE CORE
PURPOSE—E PLURIBUS UNUM

With a mission in place, the next major task was steering the ship toward those common "core beliefs," a never-ending, daily effort. This can be a challenge since charters are made up of people who choose them, not clientele dictated by district attendance boundaries and oftentimes somewhat homogenous. Implementation of a mission and vision required clear communication from the start and was then an ongoing focus on a daily basis. Much like sailing a boat, the winds and waters change constantly as the destination remains the same. From the initial recruiting of all stakeholders, including teachers, families, and community partners, agreement on the mission was essential to bring cohesion to the effort.

Whereas traditional principals do not typically have the luxury (or burden) of selecting their learning community, they typically do have one in place when they arrive. This typically even includes a mission statement. However, ask any traditional teacher (or principal) to recite their schools' mission statement and many would be remiss to recall those seemingly important words. In other words, most traditional schools have a ready-made student population and regardless of the mission (or lack thereof), they are in place. Few vote with their feet in this environment.

Charter leaders have to find their learning community members through the lens of their mission, and convince them that the jump is worth the risk. Then no matter who signs up to board the boat, no matter how diverse the thoughts and beliefs and abilities of the charter community that shows up, they must agree to head toward the same destination. They must buy-in (and continue to buy in) to the mission over time. Every charter leader interviewed emphasized the importance of this principle, of many, one.

Whether the leader had a business or education background, he or she needed to develop the skills to inspire others to become part of their vision while managing a diverse team. This seemed natural for them as they were so passionately driven at the onset; anyone wanting to be part of their team was almost preselected through buy-in to their vision in the first place. But sales and sustenance are two different strengths and maintaining the energy and excitement for the mission was critical to maintaining authentic leadership and unity.

Some of our leaders called it an ability to motivate; others talked about inspiring others, they all knew that clarity and unity toward the mission had to be relayed through hope and optimism for their communities of learners. They helped their communities feel united and emanated that failure was not an option. They were in essence making a promise to their stakeholders and their stakeholders had to believe in them to sign on and stay.

Dave Machado, with his business background called this daily maintenance of the mission "customer service" as well as just education. Joe Maimone, again coming from the business sector, mentioned being "customer-friendly" and "customer-driven." These charter leaders were exceptional listeners and were able to make all of their constituents (or customers) feel "heard."

Whether this skill involved hiring and retaining staff, extending community outreach, improving family relations, or ensuring student success and satisfaction, these leaders led with the belief that one must clearly communicate the mission and vision in every action possible each and every day. Most of the leaders insisted that they must hold high expectations related to the mission and vision, while still listening to the stakeholders, the staff, community partners, families, and students.

It was also an underlying assumption that leaders must know their people well; students, families, and community; know what they care about; know their passions and goals. The passion of the parents was of course, usually their children's well-being. The leaders had to be relationship builders with both parents and students over time to maintain their populations. How do current principal preparation programs ready candidates for getting to know their communities deeply? Teach them customer service? Teach them this level of commitment?

AMASSING THE SAILORS FOR THE SCHOOL BOAT

The students and parents came to these charter schools by choice. They heard about the schools, in some cases visited the schools, and something they heard or saw (likely the mission and the messenger delivering it) convinced them to take a risk. Obviously employing teachers that buy into a common "core belief" was also important and in almost every case, excellent instruction of some kind was critical to achieving the school goals. Consequently, our leaders all felt that getting the right people on board was essential to the success of their charter schools. They needed teachers who bought into the missions and were (or could become) excellent teachers.

Thomas and Sullivan focused on hands-on, project-based education so any stand-and-deliver teachers were not brought aboard. Machado and Maimone sought more direct instruction or mastery learning expertise in their hires. At ABS, Principal Hollis pointed out that her teachers needn't be professional level artists, they just had to embrace those with more developed arts skills than they, and welcome them into their curriculum and classrooms daily.

To continually move forward after finding and recruiting teachers and staff, leaders also needed more than just physical resources. They needed the people skills, and the know-how to retain them. They needed human resources. This did not necessarily require a particular pedigree or credential, it required people smarts. And in the schools business, unlike business schools, the instructional piece of the core belief system had to be nurtured and continually developed by the team through a focus on instructional leadership over time. Everyone was a learner, every day.

Joe Maimone tried to describe this, claiming that he "leads from the heart." He believes that motivating his staff and stakeholders is essential to growing his community. But, he pointed out that passion alone cannot support a successful charter school. He, and all of these leaders, knew that instructional leadership was as critical a piece of the equation for success as business skills or passion. In most cases, this was a research-based, data-driven approach with all stakeholders constantly seeking what resulted in improved learning for the students. They were constantly a community of learners.

LEADER AS SAIL, RUDDER, OR ANCHOR AS NEEDED

Each narrative included tales of the leader's learning curve whether through professional development, coursework, coaching, or (mostly) trial and error. They were never stagnant. Throughout the learning process; they remained anchored in the core beliefs or missions continually while managing the organizations along their journeys. Perhaps it was this constant focus and refocusing on the mission through every challenge, choice, and decision made that helped keep the work invigorating and interesting to them.

One major difference between these charter leaders and traditional public school leaders was that they created their schools from the ground up directly from a focused mission while traditional principals typically arrive at a school that already claims to have one. A lesson to future traditional leaders is to be completely confident in their own ability to buy-in to the school mission and keep it front and center in every action or decision made to provide strength and build trust in the school community. "Faking it" would not likely lead to the levels of success that these leaders achieved.

KNOWING WHAT YOU KNOW, LEARNING WHAT YOU CAN, AND DELEGATING AT THE RIGHT TIME (AKA NAVIGATING ROUGH WATERS)

Since charter school leaders frequently face unique challenges, some changing with every legislative session, effective leaders must develop strategies to problem-solve. This typically involves continuous learning, and then oftentimes delegating to others in the school community. Hollis of ABS shared this lesson, "Constant learning but frequent delegating; It's important to understand the many roles the charter school leader plays; from superintendent to marketing director, from instructional leader to plumber, from grant writer to disciplinarian." These skills go hand-in-hand: communicating the mission and vision, building a strong team of highly qualified and skilled staff and partners, and making the decision to delegate when appropriate.

Successful delegation involves learning the trade by investigating what is needed in a particular situation. What does the data say? What has a history of working here and what doesn't? Then the leader must know their people. Who has the best chance of achieving the best results? The leader must instill confidence in the employees and the employees must feel safe that their leader will not hang them out to dry should they fail.

This scenario was mentioned multiple times by our leaders and is a delicate human relations equation. Constituents must have the courage to take risks accompanied by the trust that they will be rescued if they fall. Considering how this could be taught impinges on other content areas altogether and begs the question of whether enough psychology content is present in principal prep programs.

The leader must lead by example in these cases as well. They should be willing to step in and step up to the challenge when nobody knows what exactly to do and no data delivers a clear choice. It means tackling the tough stuff and being willing to publicly fail. This takes courage and at times, faith. It also takes grit and persistence. Where and how do we learn to be courageous, to risk and to be willing to chance exposed failure?

The leaders also shared that they should perceive when it is best to hand the reins over to someone else in the organization who may have the expertise in a particular area and trust that they are sufficiently prepared to take the reins. Courage, passion, focus, trust, collaboration, and delegation were all critically important for these leaders and the relationship components or people skills provided the glue that held their organizations together.

THE BUCK STOPS HERE

The leader's role in each of these charter cases was pivotal to the success of their school. In fact, these narratives highlight a disproportional influence of the individual leader in their particular school and that leader's influence directly led to sustained and successful performance over the decades. The charter school leader appears to have more influence on their organization than tradition public school leaders—for better or worse.

Robin Hollis commented, "Nobody is going to bail me out." While charter leaders will surely need to delegate, according to these leaders, they will also need to understand the managerial aspects of running a charter school. Skills in finance, policy and law, and facilities management are all essential skills that must be learned and developed early on. Formal education and professional development may be resources for developing these skills; however, our leaders reminded us that being open to "on the job" learning is just as essential.

We learned that the skills needed by successful charter school leaders may be more in line with skills of a district superintendent than a traditional public school principal. These leaders need the big picture perspective and have a need to see the forest as well as the trees of schooling. Traditional principal preparation programs, they felt, were a mixed bag; some may be geared more toward managing the trees while others remained theory based.

Ironically, attention to detail and a willingness to roll up their sleeves and deal with the smallest of tasks (the trees), toilet paper in the bathrooms for instance, seemed equally important. No job is too big or too small for the effective charter leader. This comment was mentioned repeatedly by both the leaders and their stakeholders.

The charter leaders who had participated in a traditional principal preparation program all commented that while some of the curriculum was helpful, it was in no way enough or targeted sufficiently to prepare them for charter leadership. In light of the growth of charters nationwide, alternative leadership preparation programs and more specific professional development opportunities are needed to prepare future charter school leaders to be ready to meet the challenges of the charter school world, a different world than traditional public school organizations.

NATURE OF NURTURE?

Oftentimes educational leaders in school systems move from institution to institution, presumably learning lessons along the way. Some are in fact working in one particular educational setting specifically to move on to another, such as moving from a school site to a district office position somewhere else.

These leaders did not. Learn, they did! But leave, they didn't. Each of those we interviewed stayed over time, often blazing new trails, but their efforts were always firmly rooted in and for their original school community. We learned that, while they felt their greatest commitment was for the mission of the school, in actuality, it was for the students and families of the school. The relationship between these leaders and their schools more closely resembled a marriage than a courtship as with most traditional or more temporary principalships.

These charter leaders all grew professionally and personally as their schools flourished. They persevered through the difficult times, overcoming obstacles, never giving up, and their persistence paid off. As we have seen, each wore many hats depending on the situation on any given day or year or decade. Each changed and grew as the needs of the school changed and grew. This ability to sustain and thrive through flexibility combined with rock solid commitment to the mission and the children was woven through all aspects of these leaders' stories. They were more than a learning community, they were a family.

How do we teach these skills or traits? All were unanimous that having a mentor, shadowing a successful charter leader, would be the best possible learning opportunity for future leaders. They remarked that seeing the day-to-day activities of running charter schools firsthand was tremendously valuable to fully fathom the role. All of them had worked in their schools and had a more real and realistic understanding of the role. The role required a level of commitment, dedication, hard work, and even sacrifice that many cannot imagine until they are midstream. And in these cases, the word commitment was personified by specific children and families. Many school leaders, and even some charter leaders, abandon ship. None of these did and all were successful.

Success was rather loosely defined and varied by leader. Several of the schools were highly successful based on test scores. Other schools were considered "B" schools and were completely "fine with that." However, responses were all personified with specific testimonies about specific students. "Eight of our graduates are now teaching here." "Many of our students come back and tell us how well prepared they were for college."

This kind of success may not be realized in a year or two, or even three. But these leaders expressed that genuine success should be sustainable, result in significant, positive and even permanent change in students in some way. They acknowledged that this may require many years to achieve and likened the role more to parenting than directing or leading.

Ultimately, all of our interviewees, despite the diversity of backgrounds, portrayed the zeal of a missionary combined with the commitment of a marriage regarding their missions. And rather than stating that they had achieved genuine success despite their school numbers, they tended to see themselves as achieving success each and every day along their journeys. Regardless of their high test scores or long waiting lists, none of them considered themselves as having "arrived." Also, fortunately, all hoped to see educational successes improve nationwide and all welcomed future leaders to come join them as learners.

About the Authors

Maria Marsella Leahy, a lifelong learner, is passionate about being an agent of change in education. She has been both a teacher and an administrator in a variety of diverse K–12 schools, as well as faculty in higher education. Her goal is to help cultivate, in others, the tools that they need to be creative, curious lifelong learners. Over thirty years ago when she began her teaching career in a high-needs school as a second grade teacher, she knew how important it was to be the catalyst for change for her students. Whether she is working with school boards, families, graduate students, or children, her focus is always on what is best for children. She has been a teacher and administrator in a school specializing on meeting the needs of students with unique learning needs, a board of directors for a charter school whose mission is to develop health and wellness for mindful citizens, and is most currently an administrator in a parochial high school. She believes students should be in schools that meet their individual needs.

Dr. Leahy earned her decorate in Educational Leadership at the University of North Carolina, Charlotte; her dissertation title is *Characteristics and Skills of Sustained Leaders of Successful Public Charter Schools in North Carolina*. She teaches graduate classes at UNC Charlotte. She enjoys working with leaders to develop and hone leadership skills which are essential to continuing to grow and develop schools that are effective in our ever-changing world.

Dr. Leahy has published several articles and essays related to special education, school and teacher leadership, and nontraditional school leadership. She has also published a book for teacher literacy in the classroom. Dr. Leahy is involved in Girl Scouts, advocating for Girl Scouting in Title 1 schools. She spends time as a tutor, Girl Scout leader, and church outreach member working with children living in poverty. Dr. Leahy spends her leisure time on the tennis court, hiking, doing yoga, and enjoying her family, especially her granddaughter, Josie.

Rebecca Ann Shore is an associate professor in the Department of Educational Leadership at the University of North Carolina at Charlotte. Prior to UNC Charlotte, Dr. Shore worked in schools for twenty-eight years in California, Louisiana, and North Carolina; thirteen years of teaching and fifteen years in administration. Her undergraduate degree from Louisiana State University was in Music Education, and she was a choral director for ten years. Her doctoral degree in Educational Administration and Policy is from the University of Southern California and her dissertation title was *New Professional Opportunities for Teachers in the California Charter Schools.* Dr. Shore served as principal of Los Alamitos High School, a four-time National Blue Ribbon School in southern California, and in a variety of administrative roles in the Huntington Beach Union High School District.

Dr. Shore is the author of four books and the producer of two educational CD series. Her latest book, *Developing Young Minds from Conception to Kindergarten* was awarded the top ranking of "Essential" by the Association of Research Colleges & Universities. She was named the Higher Education Arts Educator of the Year in 2016 by the North Carolina Art Educators Association. Her research interests include leadership in early childhood education, charter school leadership, arts in education, and incorporating the science of learning into educational environments. Dr. Shore is the mother of two adult children and resides with her husband in Charlotte, North Carolina, where she sings in her church choir and in a local chorale.